THE AZTEC
WORLD

S M I T H S O N I A N
EXPLORING THE ANCIENT WORLD

JEREMY A. SABLOFF, Editor

THE AZTEC WORLD

By ELIZABETH HILL BOONE

St. Remy Press • Montreal

Smithsonian Books • Washington, D.C.

EXPLORING THE ANCIENT WORLD
was produced by
ST. REMY PRESS

Publisher	Kenneth Winchester
President	Pierre Léveillé
Managing Editor	Carolyn Jackson
Managing Art Director	Diane Denoncourt
Production Manager	Michelle Turbide
Administrator	Natalie Watanabe

Staff for *THE AZTEC WORLD*

Editor	Alfred LeMaitre
Art Director	Philippe Arnoldi
Picture Editor	Christopher Jackson
Researcher	Olga Dzatko
Assistant Editor	Jennifer Meltzer
Photo Assistants	Neale McDevitt
	Geneviève Monette
Illustrator	Maryse Doray
Systems Coordinator	Jean-Luc Roy
Administrative Assistant	Dominique Gagné
Indexer	Christine Jacobs
Proofreader	Garet Markvoort

THE SMITHSONIAN INSTITUTION

Secretary	Robert McC. Adams
Assistant Secretary for External Affairs	Thomas E. Lovejoy
Director, Smithsonian Institution Press	Felix C. Lowe

SMITHSONIAN BOOKS

Editor-in-Chief	Patricia Gallagher
Senior Editor	Alexis Doster III
Editors	Amy Donovan
	Joe Goodwin
Assistant Editors	Brian D. Kennedy
	Sonia Reece
Senior Picture Editor	Frances C. Rowsell
Picture Editors	Carrie F. Bruns
	R. Jenny Takacs
Picture Research	V. Susan Guardado
Production Editor	Patricia Upchurch
Business Manager	Stephen J. Bergstrom

Library of Congress Cataloging-in-Publication Data
Boone, Elizabeth Hill
   The Aztec World/ Elizabeth Hill Boone
      p. cm. — (Exploring the ancient world)
   Includes bibliographical references and index.
   ISBN 0-89599-040-7
   1. Aztecs I. Title.   II. Series.
   F1219.73.B66   1994
   972'.018—dc20   94-9830
                                                   CIP

Manufactured and printed in Canada.
First Edition

10 9 8 7 6 5 4 3 2 1

FRONT COVER PHOTO: *Mosaic decoration was a highly developed craft in Aztec times. This detail shows part of a double-headed serpent pectoral decorated with turquoise and shell mosaic.*

BACK COVER PHOTO: *The reconstructed pyramid of Santa Cecilia Acatitlan, located in a suburb of Mexico City, gives an idea of what the shrine of an Aztec temple looked like.*

CONTENTS

EDITOR'S FOREWORD

Over the centuries—from the time of the Spanish conquistadors' reports of their conquest of the Mexica to the modern day—the Aztec world has intrigued and fascinated people all over the globe. However, the rise of the Aztecs, their cultural practices, and their demise in A.D. 1521 are not well understood by much of the general public, and certain aspects of Aztec culture, such as human sacrifice and possible cannibalism, often have been distorted or sensationalized. Moreover, the reasons for the success of Hernán Cortés and his soldiers frequently have not been fully or clearly explained. Fortunately, in recent years ongoing scholarly research on the Aztecs has been made increasingly accessible to the general reader. In particular, this new volume in the *Exploring the Ancient World* series should go a long way in rectifying many misunderstandings about the Aztecs and their two centuries of florescence.

In the beautifully written and informative text that follows, Dr. Elizabeth Boone shows how one Aztec group, the Mexica, became the most powerful people in ancient Mexico, built the remarkable capital city of Tenochtitlan, and spread its economic and political influence over a vast territory in less than 200 years.

Dr. Boone shows how all aspects of Mexica society, from its social classes to its lifestyle and religious beliefs and practices, were influenced by its immediate history. She provides a useful synthesis of the early history, the entrance into the Valley of Mexico, and the initial settlement of Tenochtitlan. Dr. Boone then relates this history to the growth of Mexica power in a well-integrated discussion of the last century of Mexica development.

The strength of Dr. Boone's presentation is that it is not limited to an exposition of *what* happened in the Valley of Mexico in the 14th to early 16th centuries A.D.; it also provides some stimulating insights into *how* and *why* the Mexica developed the way they did and why they fell prey to the Spanish in A.D. 1521. This discussion has particular clarity, because it combines perspectives from historical materials (both Mexican and Spanish), archaeological research, and art historical interpretations. As Dr. Boone tellingly shows, all these sources of information are needed in order to reach any productive understanding of the Mexica and the Aztec world.

Readers of this volume will have the satisfaction of seeing many of the stereotypes about the Aztecs demolished and more supportable inferences of

Aztec behavior substituted for the outdated characterizations. They will discover that the Aztec empire was not the tightly knit political entity that one usually associates with the term "empire," but was a loose grouping of disparate peoples who paid tribute to the emperor in Tenochtitlan without being directly controlled by the capital city. Readers also will gain a new appreciation for the cultural achievements of the Aztecs and for the many disadvantages that the Mexica faced in their confrontation with the brilliant strategies of Cortés and his allies. In this regard, Dr. Boone also considers the important roles of the political alliances Cortés struck with other Mexican peoples, who supplied soldiers and food; the different modes of warfare practiced by the Spanish and by the Mexicans; and the disastrous diseases introduced by the Spanish.

Dr. Elizabeth Boone is highly qualified to write about the Aztecs. She is an internationally recognized art historian who has specialized in the study of Aztec pictorial documents and art. She received her doctorate in Pre-Columbian art history from the University of Texas at Austin and, for more than a decade, has been the Director of Pre-Columbian Studies and Curator of the Pre-Columbian Collection at Dumbarton Oaks in Washington, D.C. She has been a Paul Mellon Senior Fellow at the Center for Advanced Study in the Visual Arts at the National Gallery of Art (1993-1994) and has received the prestigious Order of the Aztec Eagle from Mexico. She is the author of *The Codex Magliabechiano and the Lost Prototype of the Magliabechiano Group* (1983) and *Incarnations of the Aztec Supernatural: The Image of Huitzilopochtli in Mexico and Europe* (1989) as well as the editor of a number of books including (among the most recent): *The Aztec Templo Mayor* (1987), *Collecting the Pre-Columbian Past* (1993), and (with Walter D. Mignolo) *Writing Without Words* (1994).

From the intellectual revelations recently produced by the exciting excavations in the Templo Mayor of Tenochtitlan to the reexaminations of Aztec art and history, ongoing Aztec research has thrown much new light on these justly famous peoples. Dr. Boone has been at the forefront of this new scholarship and shares her great knowledge of the Aztecs in the pages that follow.

Jeremy A. Sabloff
University of Pittsburgh

Cortés and his expedition first made landfall in 1519 on Cozumel Island, off the Yucatan peninsula. Some contact between the Spaniards and place, but these encounters had been fleeting and inconclusive. Cozumel's stone temples and public buildings revealed the existence of a highly

the inhabitants of Yucatan had already taken developed Mesoamerican civilization.

1

A SPLENDID WORLD APART

They were four days out of Cuba, these Spanish adventurers, when they sighted Cozumel Island, rising like a verdant crown above the crystal blue waters. Everywhere expectations were high. Hernán Cortés, their bold leader, had spoken eloquently about the riches to be found in these newly discovered lands to the west, and the seamen and soldiers who chose to join his expedition that February of 1519 all looked for excitement, glory, and wealth. Some had already sailed along these shores with

9

the two earlier expeditions the two previous years. They had tried their luck at seeking their fortune, and they had seen firsthand the peoples and the towns. They had traded for gold along the coast and had heard the promise of rich gold mines in the interior, and they also had chanced upon the victims of human sacrifice. They knew that the people in this land had markedly different customs than any of the other peoples they had encountered before in the New World. The veterans had already had a peek at the sophisticated people in whose territory they intruded; the others could only imagine.

Later, as they strode into the civic center of the island, the well-arranged masonry architecture was a surprise to those who never had been to this land. The native inhabitants of Hispañola, Cuba, and the other Caribbean islands with which the Spaniards were familiar, built simpler and more perishable structures of wood and cane, but here on the northeastern edge of Mexico, just off the coast of the Yucatan peninsula, the Spaniards realized they had entered a different world. Here they passed by the wood and cane houses of commoners to reach the heart of Cozumel, where the houses of the rulers and the public structures had both size and permanence. They marveled at the stone buildings raised on platforms around a series of plazas. All were plastered, and most were embellished with sculpted and painted designs the likes of which the Spaniards had never seen.

The adventurers immediately knew that underlying this architecture must be a sizable population organized as a hierarchical social system of commoners and elites. Unconsciously they recognized the craft specialization necessary to create these fine buildings—the architects, the stonemasons and woodcutters, the lime makers and plasterers, the sculptors and painters, the cooks and the farmers— and the social and economic structure that could coordinate the work of so many. They also knew that such buildings were created by wealth, and their hearts must have quickened at the thought of the gold these structures implied.

The temples they had heard so much about from the veterans in the group stood out clearly, for these shrines usually sat atop the highest stepped pyramids, being approached by broad stairways; and the unmistakable smell of blood was in the air.

Inside the sanctuaries, the walls were adorned with rich cloth hangings; there were chests for storing the exquisite paraphernalia of the ritual; and set all around were sculptures of animals and of animal-human combinations that were beyond imagining to Europeans. The bloody remains of a recent human sacrifice were still on the altar, over which a fearsome cult image presided. One of those soldiers who walked into that civic center that day vividly describes what it was like to come upon such a scene. Speaking of another temple in another town, Bernal Díaz del Castillo remembered: "We found two stone buildings of good workmanship, each with a flight of steps leading up to a kind of altar, and on those altars were evil-looking idols, which were their gods. Here we found five Indians who had been sacrificed to them on that very night. Their chests had been struck open and their arms and thighs cut off, and the walls of these buildings were covered with blood. All this amazed us greatly."

The whole of the ceremonial and civic center was disconcertingly quiet. All the inhabitants of Cozumel, save for the few who hid, had fled as soon as they saw the Spaniards dock in their port. They had heard about the bloody skirmishes that other coastal peoples had had with these intruders the previous two years, and they wanted nothing to do with the dangerous men who had just disembarked. Despite the blood on their altars, the inhabitants of Cozumel did not desire to eradicate the foreigners; they only wished to avoid them. They returned to their town only after the Spaniards assured them of their peaceful intent.

Once the inhabitants returned, the Spaniards learned that Cozumel was not an isolated or independent entity. Instead, the polity was tied into a vast political, religious, and economic network involving countless other cities and towns. It was part of the cultural region we now call Mesoamerica, which embraced Mexico, Guatemala, Belize, and parts of Honduras and El Salvador. Cozumel itself stood out from many other towns because it was a pilgrimage center, whose religious cults attracted many worshippers from across the Yucatan peninsula. These pilgrims regularly filled the plazas and courtyards in front of the temples. The large canoes that traveled up and down the eastern coast of the Yucatan peninsula relied on Cozumel's fine port; they linked the island economically to a good part of eastern Mesoamerica. The Spaniards also saw how Cozumel, even though it lay on the very eastern edge of the Yucatan, was tied intellectually to the rest of Mesoamerica. Swift messengers carried news to and from distant centers, and knowledge recorded in painted books circulated widely among nobles and scribes trained to read and interpret the pictorial writing. At Cozumel, Cortés and his compatriots got their first sense of the great complexity of the cultural landscape they had entered.

By the time Cortés had left Cozumel, sailing westward along the Gulf Coast, and had arrived along the coast of Veracruz, he had learned that much of the land he skirted was dominated by a great empire, whose capital lay to the west over the mountains. The coastal inhabitants, when asked the source of their gold and their jewels, had consistently replied "Culhua" and "Mexica" and had pointed westward. They pronounced it *Kól-wah* and *May-shé-kah*, and the Spaniards wrote it as Culhua and Mexica, transcribing the *wah* as *hua* and the *she* as *xi* according to the way they usually spelled these sounds then. By these words, the coastal informants meant the people we popularly call Aztecs, who knew themselves to be Culhua-Mexica:

In October 1518, Hernán Cortés was appointed by the governor of Cuba to lead an expedition of exploration and discovery on the American mainland. A native of the city of Medellín in Extremadura, Spain, Cortés had left his native country at age 19 to seek his fortune in the new Caribbean colonies and had won favor for his role in the conquest of Cuba.

Culhua referring to their ancestral links with the ancient civilized peoples of Culhuacan, and Mexica being the name they adopted along their long migration into the Central Valley of Mexico.

Cortés did not then know the full meaning of these words, but he understood well that they referred to the people whose empire controlled much of these lands. It was also evident that many of the coastal people feared them greatly. Thus, Cortés discovered that the wealth he sought was tied to the imperial power of the Culhua-Mexica. He hoped to approach it through Veracruz, where an earlier expedition had encountered one edge of the empire's vast domain.

He was in luck. Cortés had barely set foot on the beach at Veracruz when he was greeted by two of the governors of that land, servants of the imperial lord Moctezuma. They had come, at their emperor's request, to see what kind of strangers had once again landed on these shores. They also brought food for the Spaniards, and wood for shelters, and, to Cortés' great delight, they brought a chest filled with precious gifts—beautifully worked gold objects, jewelry, and cloths made of cotton and feathers, which, according to the conqueror Bernal Díaz, were "a marvelous sight."

The Spaniards were impressed by these governors, who were so confident in their command and who so clearly had great resources at their disposal. Accompanied by retainers and aides, their bearing was exceedingly proud. They spoke a beautiful and melodious language, Nahuatl. They wore elegant cloaks of white cotton and finely woven loincloths, all richly decorated with embroidered patterns and borders; even their leather sandals were richly made. Artfully crafted necklaces, ear-ornaments, wrist bands, and leg bands of precious materials adorned their bodies, and gold lip-plugs pierced the skin just below their lower lips, further enhancing their profiles. They carried feather fans and flowers, and took the opportunity to perfume Cortés and the men around him with incense.

Bernal Díaz recalled that one of the governors "brought with him some of those skilled painters they have in Mexico and...gave them instructions to make realistic full-length portraits of Cortés and all his captains and soldiers, also to draw the ships, sails, and horses, Doña Marina and [the Spaniard] Aguilar [interpreters whom Cortés acquired earlier], and even the two greyhounds. The cannon and cannonballs, and indeed the whole of our army, were faithfully portrayed, and the drawings were taken to Montezuma [Moctezuma]." Indeed, one of the governors himself conveyed these paintings, which were executed on cloth sheets or bark-paper scrolls, overland to the magnificent imperial capital of Mexico-Tenochtitlan, now Mexico City, where he gave his emperor a complete account of the foreigners.

The governor soon returned with other gifts from Moctezuma, gifts so fabulous that Bernal Díaz could still describe them 50 years later:

> The first was a disk in the shape of the sun, as big as a cart wheel and made of very fine gold. It was a marvelous thing engraved with many sorts of fig-

The Aztec empire extended from the Gulf of Mexico to the Pacific Ocean and from what is now north-central Mexico to Guatemala (off the map to the right). From the capital of Tenochtitlan, in the heavily urbanized Valley of Mexico, Aztec power radiated through the empire by means of alliances, tribute, and trade. The inset map at top right shows the modern nations that today compose Mesoamerica.

ures and, as those who afterwards weighed it reported, was worth more than ten thousand pesos. There was another larger disk of brightly shining silver in the shape of the moon, with other figures on it, and this was worth a great deal for it was very heavy. ...[A] helmet [was] full of small grains of gold, just as they come from the mines and worth three thousand pesos. The gold in the helmet was worth more than twenty thousand pesos to us, because it proved to us that there were good mines in the country. Next came twenty golden ducks, of fine workmanship and very realistic, some ornaments in the shape of their native dogs, many others in the shapes of jaguars, pumas, and monkeys, ten necklaces of very fine workmanship, some pendants, twelve arrows and a strung bow, and two rods like staffs of justice twenty inches long, all modeled in fine gold. Next they brought crests of gold, plumes of rich green feathers, silver crests, some fans of the same material, models of deer in hollow gold, and many other things that I cannot remember...and after this came thirty loads of beautiful cotton cloth of various patterns, decorated with feathers of many colors, and so many other things that I cannot attempt to describe them.

Cortés accepted the gifts with delight. His long dream of gaining riches in the New World was at last on the verge of coming true, for these gifts exceeded even his great expectations. They were like the precious treasures he and his men had read about in the chivalrous romance novels so popular at the time—fabulous objects of exquisite and curious manufacture, unlike anything they knew. Upon seeing such fine gifts, Cortés could imagine the great wealth of the capital from where these tokens were sent. He was more anxious than ever to visit the imperial seat of Tenochtitlan and to meet its supreme ruler.

But the distant Moctezuma had other desires. The Aztec emperor had instructed his governors to dissuade Cortés from journeying further. He had no intention of granting Cortés an audience; his governors told the Spaniard to take these gifts, gather his men, and leave these lands. Days later, when Cortés showed no signs of leaving, Moctezuma sent orders to break off all conversations with the Spaniards. The inhabitants of the area and the servants of Moctezuma immediately ceased coming to the Spanish camp, where food supplies quickly dwindled and a growing sense of isolation began to set in. This was Cortés' first experience with the negative side of the imperial control. His desire to journey inland was strong, but he lacked provisions and any knowledge of the countryside. His position, squatting precariously on the edge of a now-hostile empire, seemed untenable—his dreams of conquest and glory stymied.

Then some Totonac messengers arrived, and everything seemed to change. Cortés learned from them a most valuable fact, and this was to change his perspective entirely and affect his actions from that time onward. He learned that Moctezuma's great empire had inherent weakness. As Bernal Díaz tells it, the Totonac messengers had been sent by their local lord who had heard about the Spaniards' brave deeds and their presence on the beach, and who wished to ally himself with such valiant men. The

The principal temple-pyramid at Cempoala is one of the most imposing remnants of Totonac culture. The city was founded around A.D. 1200 but came under Aztec control about 1460. Cortés first made contact with Moctezuma's representatives near Cempoala, north of the present-day city of Veracruz. In 1519, the city was a flourishing center with more than 30,000 inhabitants. Its population declined after the Spanish Conquest; today it is a small village.

Totonacs would have come sooner, but for their fear of the people from the imperial capital. "As this conversation went on, Cortés learned that Montezuma had opponents and enemies, which greatly delighted him."

When Cortés went to visit this Totonac lord, who ruled the nearby city of Cempoala and its countryside, he came to understand the situation more clearly. Here were a separate people with their own cultural traditions and ethnic identity, who spoke neither the Maya language of Cozumel and the Yucatan peninsula nor the Nahuatl or Mexican language of Moctezuma's governors, but rather spoke their own Totonac tongue. Cempoala was the largest city the Spaniards had yet encountered, for it had long been a major power along the Gulf Coast, but it had recently come under Aztec domination and was chafing at the newly applied harness. As Cortés offered his services and support, the Totonac lord aired his troubles. Bernal Díaz recalls how the Totonac ruler "heaved a deep sigh and broke into bitter complaints against the great Montezuma and his governors, saying that the Mexican prince had recently brought him into subjection, had taken away all his golden jewelry, and so grievously oppressed him and his people that they could do nothing except obey him, since he was lord over many cities and countries, and ruler over countless vassals and armies of warriors."

At the other Totonac cities and towns in the area, the Spaniards heard the same thing: complaints against Moctezuma, who demanded the sons and daughters of the local nobility for service in the capital city or, worse, for the sacrificial stone, and whose tax-gatherers extracted heavy tribute.

Beyond the Totonac sphere, there were other polities who equally feared and despised their Culhua-Mexica overlords.

Cortés learned, too, that there were towns, cities, and entire nations that had not yet been brought under the imperial yoke and thus paid no tribute to Mexico. He heard about the Tlaxcalans, old allies of the Totonacs and deadly enemies of the Culhua-Mexica, and about the peoples of other areas who fiercely kept their independence by almost constant warfare against the Mexica. He saw that the political landscape of this territory was not monochromatic; instead, it was richly variegated with ethnically distinct peoples who were not universally content to be part of the Culhua-Mexica empire and who thus just might be persuaded to side with Cortés against Moctezuma if the situation was right. Cortés learned that Moctezuma had great forces of warriors ready to quell uprisings in the provinces and posted large armies on the frontiers. This permanent state of armed readiness throughout the empire suggested to Cortés that the empire, for all its splendor and might, was internally unstable and potentially could be fragmented. He was very pleased with all this news.

As Cortés and his compatriots traveled onward into the interior, they were careful to avoid the lands and cities controlled by imperial forces and to seek allies along the route. During the long months of their journey, they climbed from the humid tropical lowlands of the coast into the rugged, drier terrain of the central Mexican highlands, crossing through cold, high, mountain passes. The more they heard about Moctezuma's power, the more they desired to see the fabled city of Mexico-Tenochtitlan, described in glorious terms by all who spoke of it. They knew it to be an island city, situated in a lake rich with flora and fauna, the cosmopolitan center of commerce and power, and wealthy beyond imagining. By the time they and their growing number of indigenous allies entered the Valley of Mexico, they were well-prepared for a magnificent city. Still, the wonder of the place overpowered them.

THE ISLAND CITY

Bernal Díaz could recall it vividly—that day in November of 1519, when the Spaniards and their followers approached the city, and elaborately dressed dignitaries came from Moctezuma to meet them. These dignitaries had brought many retainers with them, and, as people from many towns had come out to see the Spaniards, all the roads were full.

> We came to a broad causeway [a road built up from the shallow lake bottom] and continued our march.... And when we saw all those cities and villages built in the water, and other great towns on dry land, and that straight and level causeway leading to Mexico, we were astounded. These great towns and pyramids and buildings rising from the water, all made of stone, seemed like an enchanted vision from the tale of Amadis [a popular chival-

The city of Tenochtitlan stood on an island in Lake Texcoco, one of a chain of five lakes in the Valley of Mexico. Causeways linked the city to the mainland, and an aqueduct supplied Tenochtitlan with fresh water. In the center of this detail from a reconstruction by Miguel Covarrubias, the main routes converge on Tenochtitlan's ceremonial precinct, site of the major temples and palaces of the Aztec rulers. At the far left is the ritual center of Tlatelolco, commercial heart of the empire and site of Tenochtitlan's famous market.

rous romance novel of the day]. Indeed, some of our soldiers asked whether it was not all a dream. It is not surprising therefore that I should write in this vein. It was all so wonderful that I do not know how to describe this first glimpse of things never heard of, seen or dreamed of before.

... With a large escort of these great *Caciques* [lords], [we] followed the causeway, which is eight yards wide and goes so straight to the city of Mexico that I do not think it curves at all. Wide though it was, it was so crowded with people that there was hardly room for them all. Some were going to Mexico and others coming away, besides those who had come out to see us, and we could hardly get through the crowds that were there. For the towers and *cues* [pyramids] were full, and they came in canoes from all parts of the lake. No wonder, since they had never seen horses or men like us before!

With such wonderful sights to gaze on we did not know what to say, or if this was real that we saw before our eyes. On the land side there were great cities, and on the lake many more. The lake was crowded with canoes. At intervals along the causeway there were many bridges, and before us was the great city of Mexico.

We marched along...[until] we were met by many more *Caciques* and dignitaries in very rich cloaks. The different chieftains wore different brilliant liveries, and the causeways were full of them. Montezuma had sent these great *Caciques* in advance to receive us. ...the great Montezuma...approached in a rich litter, accompanied by other great lords and feudal *Caciques* who owned vassals. When we came near to Mexico, at a place where there were some other small towers, the great Montezuma descended from his litter, and these other great *Caciques* supported him beneath a marvelously rich canopy of green feathers, decorated with gold work, silver, pearls, and jades, which hung from a sort of border. It was a marvelous sight. The great Montezuma was magnificently clad, in their fashion, and wore sandals...the soles of which are of gold and the upper parts ornamented with precious stones. And the four lords who supported him were richly clad also in garments that seem to have been kept ready for them on the road so that they could accompany their master. For they had not worn clothes like this when they came out to receive us. There were four other great *Caciques* who carried the canopy above their heads, and many more lords who walked before the great Montezuma, sweeping the ground on which he was to tread, and laying down cloaks so that his feet should not touch the earth. Not one of these chieftains dared to look him in the face. All kept their eyes lowered most reverently except those four lords, his nephews, who were supporting him.

Who could now count the multitude of men, women, and boys in the streets, on the rooftops and in canoes on the waterways, who had come out to see us? It was a wonderful sight and, as I write, it all comes before my eyes as if it had happened only yesterday.

The Spaniards entered a city much larger than any most of them had seen. In 1519, Seville, a bustling commercial center and the jumping-off point for travel to the New World, was the largest city most of the conquerors knew; it had 60,000 inhabitants. London boasted a population of only 50,000. But the Mexica capital of Mexico-Tenochtitlan had at least 150,000 inhabitants on the island city alone; it was surrounded by lakeside cities that swelled the population of the valley to 1,000,000 or more. Only Paris and Constantinople, with populations of over 300,000, were comparable. It is no wonder that Bernal Díaz was impressed by the crowds.

He and his companions were impressed, too, with the beauty and good organization of the city. Days after their arrival, Moctezuma escorted Cortés and his captains on a tour of the temple complex and marketplace of the sister city of Tlatelolco, long since incorporated by the larger polity of Mexico-Tenochtitlan. To reach the temple pyramid, they passed through several courts and enclosures that Bernal Díaz thought to be larger than the great Plaza at Salamanca. "These courts were surrounded by a double masonry wall and paved, like the whole place, with very large smooth white flagstones. Where these stones were absent everything was whitened and polished, indeed the whole place was so clean that there was not a straw or a grain of dust to be found there."

They arrived at the great temple and ascended more than 100 steps to the top:

The top of the *cue* formed an open square on which stood something like a platform, and it was here that the great stones stood on which they placed the poor Indians for sacrifice. Here also was a massive image like a dragon, and other hideous figures, and a great deal of blood that had been spilled that day.... Then Montezuma took [Cortés] by the hand and told him to look at his great city and all the other cities standing in the water, and the many others on the land round the lake; and he said that if Cortés had not had a good view of the great market-place he could see it better from where he now was. So we stood there looking, because that huge accursed *cue* stood so high that it dominated everything. We saw the three causeways that led into Mexico.... We saw the fresh water which came from [the hill of] Chapultepec to supply the city, and the bridges that were constructed at intervals on the causeways so that the water could flow in and out from one part of the lake to another. We saw a great number of canoes, some coming with provisions and others returning with cargo and merchandise.... We saw *cues* and shrines in these cities that looked like gleaming white towers and castles: a marvelous sight. All the houses had flat roofs, and on the causeways were other small towers and shrines built like fortresses.

Having examined and considered all that we had seen, we turned back to the great market and the swarm of people buying and selling. The mere murmur of their voices talking was loud enough to be heard more than three miles away. Some of our soldiers who had been in many parts of the world, in Constantinople, in Rome, and all over Italy, said that they had never seen a market so well laid out, so large, so orderly, and so full of people.

THE AZTEC QUESTION

For almost 100 years, from 1427 to 1521, the Aztec empire controlled much of civilized Mesoamerica–that expanse of Mexico, Guatemala, Belize, and western parts of Honduras and Salvador whose people inhabited a world of shared cultural traditions. Even those areas of Mesoamerica that had not come under Aztec rule still had to contend with the dominant Aztec presence. We use the term Aztec to mean the Nahuatl-speaking people of the empire, and we use the term Culhua-Mexica, or more simply Mexica, when we mean those who built and inhabited the imperial capital of Mexico-Tenochtitlan. These Mexica had come on the scene late in civilized Mesoamerica, migrating down from the rough, arid wilderness of northwestern Mexico in the 14th century to settle among the cultured peoples who for centuries had farmed the fertile valleys of central Mexico. In less than 100 years, these aggressive people had conquered, married into, and allied themselves with the existing powers to become the masters of Mesoamerica. Along the way, they had acquired knowledge, refinement, and culture.

The Spaniards who came to know the Aztecs and the other ethnic groups of Mesoamerica recognized people much like themselves. Here in this ancient land, which the Spaniards had only recently discovered for themselves and had only just learned to call America, was a world of farmers, fishermen, workers, seamen, artists, and merchants; a world of wives and mothers, cooks, spinners, and weavers; a world of warriors, priests and priestesses, kings and queens, and emperors. Yet the civilization the Spaniards encountered here had developed totally independent of any recent influence from Europe or Asia. It was a separate world from theirs, a world apart. The technology was different, and the ways of doing things were accordingly different. Lacking draft animals, the Mesoamericans relied instead on human porters. They knew the wheel and used it for toys, but not for vehicles; nor did they rely on the potter's wheel. They were exquisite workers of gold, silver, and copper, but did not alloy steel. They were great agriculturists, healers, and astronomers, but they failed to develop the kind of scientific and mechanical technology that ushered in the Age of Exploration in Europe. They wrote with pictures and images instead of with alphabetic letters and words.

The Aztecs had built for themselves a great and powerful empire, one that occupied the same niche in North and Central America that the Inca empire did in South America. These two indigenous American empires paralleled each other in time but never met, although their rulers must have known about the other's distant presence. Both proved to be equally fragile once European invaders upset the delicate balance of their worlds.

The questions the Aztecs pose to us are questions of why and how. How did the great Aztec empire come to be? How did this relatively small ethnic group called the Mexica come to power and so quickly dominate all around them? How did their culture reach the great sophistication it did, to astonish even the hardened and veteran world-travelers among the Spanish contingent? What held the empire together, and why did it fragment so quickly once a serious European presence was felt? Within two years of Cortés' entry into Mexico-Tenochtitlan, he and his allies burned the city to the ground and accepted the surrender of the Aztec emperor.

Perhaps the biggest question focuses on the bloody and terrible practice of human sacrifice. The Spaniards must have asked themselves, as we do today, how humans who seem so much like us in so many ways could have practiced human sacrifice on such a vast scale. There is no doubt that the Aztecs raised to unprecedented heights the custom of cutting out the still-beating hearts of human victims and offering these hearts and the blood to their gods. The conquerors, and the Europeans who followed them to Mexico, all describe gory scenes of sacrifice. Bernal Díaz, vivid as always, speaks of temple walls "so caked with blood and the floor so bathed in it that the stench was worse than that of any slaughter-house in Spain," adding, "They had offered that idol five hearts from the day's sacrifices."

The custom of human sacrifice by heart extraction was an ancient one in Mesoamerica, dating from about 1000 B.C. in Olmec times, according to the evidence we have from relief carvings on stone. Maya rulers of A.D. 300-900 were known to draw their own blood and offer human sacrifices as well, as did their contemporaries in other parts of Mesoamerica. But the subsequent Post-Classic peoples, and especially the Aztecs, raised the practice to a central cultural statement. We ask ourselves why.

The answers to these questions lie within the structures and nuances of Aztec life. The Aztecs came to power because it was in their character and because circumstances allowed it. Their empire fell because of the particular nature of its structure, and because Cortés understood and played to this struc-

The Aztec custom of sacrificing living human victims to the gods by heart extraction shocked the Spanish, but the practice had a long history in Mesoamerica. This detail from the *Codex Magliabechiano* shows a priest cutting out the heart of a sacrificial victim at the top of a bloodstained temple-pyramid. After the Conquest, ethnographic treatises like the *Codex Magliabechiano* were produced by Aztec painters under the direction of Spanish friars. These codices, as well as painted histories and almanacs, make up the most fertile sources of information on Aztec life and religion.

tural weakness. Even human sacrifice, as horrific as it remains, is understandable within the context of Aztec beliefs in the composition and working of the cosmos, and the place of humans within it.

RESOURCES FOR UNDERSTANDING THE AZTEC WORLD

Those of us who seek to understand the structures and nuances of Aztec life are fortunate to have a great range of resources on which to draw. The Aztecs left an impressive archaeological record, with sites scattered across Mesoamerica. Archaeologists have been excavating and analyzing these sites for more than a century, reading the broad patterns of Aztec life from the great sculptures, the complex architectural features, and the fragmentary sherds of both finely painted and domestic pottery they have found. Many of the details of Aztec life and thought, and especially those beliefs and customs not so likely to be revealed archaeologically, have been found by historians in the written record.

Unlike the Classic Maya, whose political institutions and stone cities declined long before Europeans arrived in Mexico, the Aztecs were at their imperial height when the Spaniards came to explore their lands. And the Spaniards loved the written word; seemingly at every opportunity, they wrote letters home about their explorations, and they penned chronicles, histories, and encyclopedias about the Aztecs. The Aztecs, of course, had always compiled their own histories, calendars, and records. Some of these indigenous writings have survived, either in the pictorial form in which they were originally set down, or in the alphabetic form into which they were later translated. Thus, an incredibly rich corpus of ethnohistorical sources supplements the more sketchy archaeological record.

The written record for the Aztecs begins practically with the Spanish arrival. Three months after Cortés landed on the beach at Veracruz and before he started to march inland, he sat down to write a letter to his monarch, Charles V. This famous first letter telling about his expedition and first encounter with Moctezuma's governors was later followed by four other letters which detailed his conquest of Mexico. These letters were a sensation in Europe. Cortés' words were printed and circulated (almost as a serialization: "The Conquest of Mexico"!) and avidly read by a wide audience hungry for news from the New World. Soon, Cortés' secretary, Francisco Lopéz de Gómara, wrote a unified account of the Conquest, published in 1552; accounts by other conquerors followed. The best known and most captivating of them all is *The True History of the Conquest of New Spain*, written by Cortés' loyal lieutenant Bernal Díaz del Castillo, who in his old age recalled the brave feats and wondrous sights of his youth.

Official chroniclers of the Spanish crown also were quick to describe the people and lands of Mexico. Peter Martyr d'Anghiera, an Italian humanist and man of letters, provided Europe with a running account of the discoveries and conquests from 1493 to 1525; his *Decades*, as his account was titled, was even more widely read than that of Cortés. The *Decades* remains an important record because, although Peter Martyr did not visit America, he interviewed many of the returning conquerors, and he had access to all the official reports.

In Mexico, the mendicant friars soon took up the challenge of describing the native peoples and culture. These friars—Franciscans, Dominicans, and Augustinians, who were united only by their vow of poverty—had come to Mexico soon after the Conquest to convert the vast heathen population to Christianity. Frustrated by their lack of knowledge of the customs and practices they sought to eradicate, the friars began to record Aztec thought and culture. They interviewed those old nobles and priests who survived the Conquest, and they commissioned Aztec painters to recreate the ancient images. Through this process, between about 1530 and 1580, they created encyclopedias of Aztec culture, with an emphasis on religion but with good coverage of the history and the lifeways of the people.

The most zealous and knowledgeable of these early ethnographers were the Franciscan fathers Andrés de Olmos, Toribio de Benavente (who was called Motolinía, "the poor one," because of his poverty), and, slightly later, Bernardino de Sahagún. Although most of Olmos' writings have been lost, he left behind the first grammar of the Nahuatl language and an important collection of Aztec orations; he may also have been responsible for several of the anonymous cosmogonies and cultural encyclopedias that have survived. From Motolinía comes an early history of the Franciscan conversion effort in Mexico, prefaced by a long account of Aztec history and replete with details on Aztec culture. Sahagún's magnificent ethnography survived intact; known as the *Florentine Codex* (the original is now housed in Florence) or the *General History of the Things of New Spain*, its 12 books treat a broad range of Aztec culture from religion and philosophy to the flora and fauna of the land. Like Olmos, Sahagún wrote in Nahuatl as well as Spanish.

Although the other mendicant orders produced fewer major ethnographers, the Dominican father Diego Durán stands out. His *History of the Indies of New Spain* remains a major account of Aztec political history, religion, and the calendar.

The friars were not alone in their researches into the Aztec past, for the Spanish government in Mexico also took an official interest. The Spanish Crown, in particular, wanted to know all about Aztec government, about the population, and about the tax and tribute Moctezuma received from his vassals. This was a practical interest, for the Spanish king needed information about the lands and peoples he newly governed, and he especially wanted to know the levels of tribute he could expect. Spanish administrators in Mexico also sought economic information on the local level. Thus, tax and tribute rolls, censuses, maps, and other administrative records have come down to us.

All of these documents stem from European interests, and most represent the European view of the Aztecs. If they were pictorials, however, or had a large pictorial component, the painters were native-trained artists who generally worked in their traditional style. Thus indigenous Aztec imagery and presentation survived within the covers of Spanish-commissioned documents.

Documents that represent purely the Aztec point of view have endured also. A small number of Pre-Columbian painted books—15, in fact—survived the devastation of the Conquest and the intervening centuries. They are almanacs and guides for living that came from outside the imperial heartland, but some Mixtec genealogical histories from Oaxaca and some Maya codices survived also. In the years after the Conquest, the manuscript-painting tradition continued despite the Spanish presence. Some of these colonial pictorials, which speak directly from the perspective of the conquered Aztecs and tell their side of the story, have come down to us. They include magnificent pictorial almanacs like the *Codex Borbonicus,* and painted histories of the Aztec migration and the growth of the empire, such as the *Codex Boturini* and *Codex Mexicanus*; as well as histories that continue beyond the Conquest to record the new colonial order, such as the *Tira de Tepechpan* and *Codex en Cruz.* So far, these native postconquest histories and almanacs are anonymous because their painters' identities have not been discovered.

When the native historians stopped writing pictorially and took up the European way of writing alphabetically, they tended to sign their works and to speak of themselves. We therefore know their names. They produced chronicles and histories much like their Spanish counterparts, except that they told the stories of their own people from their own points of view and often with an underlying indigenous structure. Because some of these writings have survived, we can still read the accounts of such mestizo historians as Fernando de Alva Ixtlilxochitl and Hernando Alvarado Tezozomoc, who traced their descent from noble Aztec families.

All of these documents have their own points of view, and all were created for specific purposes. Cortés wrote his letters to justify his conquest of Mexico against the express orders of the Cuban governor; Sahagún was interested in the Aztecs as bearers of high culture but also as potential converts; and the *Tira de Tepechpan* sets out to validate the independent status of Tepechpan as a city-state. Each document, therefore, tells its own story in its own way for its own

The excavation of the Templo Mayor, located behind Mexico City's Metropolitan Cathedral, has exposed the heart of the Aztec empire. The discoveries made during the excavations, which began in 1978, have led archaeologists to revise many long-accepted ideas about the Aztecs.

The Stone of Tizoc was discovered
under Mexico City's central plaza in
1791. The massive stone was carved during the short and unsuccessful reign of
Tizoc (1481-1486). On top of the stone,
the sun disk occupies the heavens.
The sides depict military campaigns
by Tizoc who is repeatedly victorious in
a series of ritual "captive" scenes, as
shown below. The scenes are framed
with masks of the earth god at the
bottom and "night-eyes" representing
stars in a sky band above.

purpose. In creating each document, the authors have selected what they choose to stress. They all enhance one thing over another; they embellish, and they all omit what is extraneous to their purpose. Thus none of the sources can tell us everything we might want to know about the Aztecs, and some can mislead us if we are gullible. The challenge for the reader, then, is to recognize the natural biases and intentions of the authors, to sort out the elaborations and omissions, in order to piece together an accurate picture.

The documentary sources give us part of the story of the Aztec world, a richly detailed part. For the rest, however, we turn to the archaeological record: the material remains of Aztec civilization itself as they have been uncovered and their patterns interpreted.

The Spaniards made every effort to destroy the physical heart of the Aztec empire and wipe away all traces of its religion. They burned Tenochtitlan to the ground, toppled its statues, and used its great temple-pyramids as quarries for stones to build the new cathedral and new colonial city. Throughout Mexico in subsequent centuries, Aztec sites were abandoned or were buried under colonial cities and towns. As foundations were dug for new buildings, great fragments of ancient sculptures would be raised from the earth. Up until the end of the 18th

Archaeologist Leopoldo Batres was the first Mexican to explore seriously what lay beneath the urban landscape of modern Mexico City. When diggers putting a sewer line behind the Metropolitan Cathedral in 1900 trenched into the Templo Mayor, Batres launched a hasty salvage excavation to save and record what he could. The materials he unearthed were pictured and described in a book entitled *Archaeological Explorations in Escalerillas Street*, a publication that marked a turning point in Mexico's awareness of its past. This collection of artifacts includes stone blades, shells, ceremonial masks, jewelry, and stone sculptures.

century, they were simply reburied or piled up at the street-corners, or sometimes they were reworked and incorporated into the new structures.

This pattern changed in 1790, when workers digging out a canal at the corner of the Zócalo (central plaza) of Mexico City unearthed two monuments of stupendous size and importance. One was the famous Stone of the Sun, popularly called the Aztec Calendar Stone and the best known of all Aztec sculptures. The other was the great Coatlicue, that horrifying image of the mother of the gods who wears a necklace of hearts and severed hands and a skirt of intertwined rattlesnakes. A year later workers found and raised the Stone of Tizoc, a third imperial monument, which displays the victories claimed by the Aztec ruler Tizoc. The stones were not reburied as they would earlier have been; instead, they were now subjected to scientific scrutiny and historical analysis. On the eve of its independence from Spain, Mexico was discovering its glorious Aztec past.

There followed in the 19th century a number of explorations of Pre-Columbian ruins outside the capital city. Most predated the period of Aztec hegemony, but Aztec sculptures continued to be dug up from time to time. They were now usually shuttled off to the newly founded National Museum of Anthropology.

In Mexico City, in 1900, a sewer line being dug behind the Metropolitan Cathedral trenched into the buried ruins of the main Aztec temple, the Templo Mayor, although the diggers did not know what they had struck at the time. Leopoldo Batres, Mexico's first archaeologist, quickly put together a salvage excavation to save and record what he could; he worked practically alone and without support, but his publication, *Archaeological Explorations in Escalerillas Street*, became a turning point for Aztec archaeology: It marked the beginning of serious excavation of Aztec remains. Thirteen years later, Manuel Gamio followed with more excavation in the area of the Templo Mayor using the new technique of stratigraphic archaeology to establish the relative chronology of the features and artifacts.

After 1900, the excavation and study of Aztec archaeological remains increased rapidly. Toward the edges of the metropolitan capital, the ceremonial center of Tenayuca was excavated, as was the ritual precinct of Tlatelolco, the very district where Moctezuma had taken Cortés and his

Electrical workers uncovered the Stone of Coyolxauhqui in 1978, a chance discovery that led to the full excavation of the Templo Mayor. The massive disk, nearly 11 feet (3.26 meters) across, shows the slain and dismembered sister of Huitzilopochtli, the principal god of the Aztecs.

captains for a view of his city. Farther afield, surveys and excavations of provincial Aztec sites broadened the archaeological base. The surface survey of the Valley of Mexico conducted in the 1970s by William Sanders, Jeffrey Parsons, and Robert Santley stands out for the detailed picture it gives of the settlement pattern and the population through time.

Back in the dense heart of Mexico City, archaeologists regularly recorded artifacts uncovered when buildings were torn down and pits dug. In this vein, the construction of the Mexico City subway in the 1960s called for much salvage work. An entire temple was even found—and left preserved—beneath the entrance to the Pino Suárez subway station. Repair to the foundations of the Cathedral in the 1970s gave the opportunity to explore there. Aztec archaeology within Mexico City tended to be a localized affair, however, with the purpose of recording what was about to be destroyed or

Unearthed during the construction of Mexico City's subway system, the small temple pyramid dedicated to the Aztec wind god Ehecatl-Quetzalcoatl is today surrounded by the bustle of Pino Suárez station. In 1519, the first meeting between Cortés and Moctezuma took place near this temple.

buried again by construction. As a result, many of the interesting archaeological questions could be addressed only by those working outside the city.

This all changed in 1978, when diggers for the Mexico City power company hit what was soon revealed to be a huge circular disk carved in relief. With traces of its original polychrome paint still on it, the disk bore the vanquished and dismembered image of Coyolxauhqui, the enemy sister of the principal Aztec god. This discovery, just steps from the apse of the Cathedral, was as dramatic as the discovery of the Calendar Stone and Coatlicue must have been nearly 200 years before, for the archaeologists all knew that the workers had found the ancient Templo Mayor. Mexican President Manuel Lopéz Portilla came to see the great stone and declared that the Aztec Templo Mayor should be excavated at last. From 1978 until 1982, the Templo Mayor excavations, coordinated by Eduardo Matos Moctezuma, uncovered the ritual heart of the Aztec empire. Public as well as scholarly attention focused on the metropolitan Aztecs. Newspapers and magazines carried the story internationally. The Coyolxauhqui image appeared on the covers of the Mexico City phone books and on Mexican bank notes.

The excavations also gave new impetus to Aztec research, which had lagged behind Maya and Oaxacan studies in previous decades. Suddenly scholarly conferences, lectures, exhibitions, and new publications focused on the Aztecs and the Templo Mayor; a new Templo Mayor museum was opened. Now outside of Mexico City, more archaeologists than ever are digging Aztec sites. More scholars from a wide range of disciplines—including anthropology, history, art history, religious studies, archaeoastronomy, and ethnobotany—are working comparatively to integrate the archaeological and documentary records. Although analysis of the excavated materials still continues, already the findings from the Templo Mayor and subsequent excavations are changing the way we think about the Aztecs. For all that has been written about the Aztecs by the conquerors, chroniclers, and native historians, the archaeological record still holds some surprises.

When recounting the story of their origin, the Mexica would talk about an island town in a placid lake, which they referred to as Place of Herons, exact location (or if, indeed, it did exist), Lake Patzcuaro, west of Mexico City, with the isle of Janitzio at its center, seems to fit the description.

2
ORIGINS

The Mexica Aztecs knew they had not always lived in the Valley of Mexico. Ancient stories, painted in their history manuscripts, told of how their ancestors had come to this land, of the long and difficult journey from Aztlan, Place of Herons. Every Mexica knew the tales well, for they all had heard the elders and historians reading and interpreting the picture writings about the past, voicing the narratives in rich detail. That there were subtle differences between the many versions of the migration story did not

or Aztlan. Although experts continue to debate its

The *Codex Boturini* gives a graphic portrayal of the epic migration of the Aztecs. On the left is the island in the lake with its temple; the man in the canoe is leaving the island, and the glyph to his right shows the date: 1 Flint. The footprints chart the migration over land. The large glyph at the center contains the god Huitzilopochtli speaking to his people from a temporary shrine at Teoculhuacan. Eight tribes, each identified by a house, a place glyph, and a ruler, or "speaker," go forth led by four *teomamaque*, who carry symbols of the gods.

seem to matter. These differences only added to the enjoyment of the telling and listening, for they gave the narrators free rein to elaborate and digress. The main outline remained the same. The moral of the story and the lessons it embodied were always clear. The Mexica began their migration as a small and relatively insignificant band of uncultured people; they endured great hardships along the way, which gave them strength, toughened their resolve, and cemented their devotion to their patron god; by the time they arrived at their new homeland, they had been transformed into people destined to rule the world as it was then known.

STORIES OF THE LONG MIGRATION

Twenty or so accounts of the Mexica migration have come down to us from the 16th century. Some are purely pictorial, laying out the narrative through the arrangement of painted figures on sheets of bark paper or animal hide, just as the histories did in Pre-Columbian times. Others have alphabetic notes and texts written beside the paintings to explain them to a postconquest audience. Others still are purely textual accounts written alphabetically in the colonial period as remembrances of the old stories. Many of these textual accounts were written in the Aztecs' own language, Nahuatl; some were then translated into Spanish. We can think of these alphabetic versions, and especially the Nahuatl ones, as giving us something close to the oration of the story as it might have been voiced. The story goes thusly:

Aztlan was an island city in the middle of a lake, surrounded by reeds and marshes. Although the region around it was arid (it was probably northwest of Mexico City), at Aztlan waterbirds and fish were plentiful. There the Mexica had lived peaceably, until their patron deity commanded them to go forth to find the land of their true destiny. The year was 1 Flint in their calendar. As one of the years in their 52-year cycle, 1 Flint reoccurred every 52 years; when it did, it tended to be the year when the Mexica, throughout their history, initiated great undertakings.

Their tribal patron was Huitzilopochtli (Wit-see-low-poach-tlee), a fierce, relentless god who drove them along every step of the migration, forcing them to give up settlements and move onward if they resided in one place too long. His name derives from *huitzilin* or hummingbird (an aggressive and tenacious bird, despite its size) and *opochtli* meaning left or south (south being thought of as the left side of the sun as the sun travels from east to west).

At his direction, the Mexica canoed across the lake and began the long march of their migration, arriving first at a mythical place called Teoculhuacan, The Place of Those with Divine Ancestors. There, as at every stop along the migration, they immediately built a temple to their god and awaited his instructions.

At this point, most of the migration stories remind us that the Mexica were just one of eight Nahuatl-speaking groups who left their homeland in the arid northwest to migrate down into the fertile valleys of the central highlands of Mexico. Such other groups as the Xochimilca, the Chalca, and the Tepaneca left also, although the Mexica were the last to go. For all these peoples, the legendary origin point was the place of Seven Caves, Chicomoztoc (*Chicome* = seven, *oztoc* = cave), whence the tribal groups emerged. In some of the paintings and writings, Chicomoztoc and Aztlan are combined; in others, they are distinct. These variations show us that two truths are operating side by side here. The broader truth is that all the Nahautl-speaking peoples (even the Mexica) originally came forth from the caves of Chicomoztoc, just as the previous Mesoamerican peoples, from Olmec times onward, had emerged from caves; the more localized truth is that the Mexica came from Aztlan.

The migration was long and arduous. At each stop, the Mexica would erect a temple to Huitzilopochtli, build houses, and plant crops to sustain them. At some places they remained for many years. Sometimes Huitzilopochtli pushed them onward early, driving them forth even before their harvest came in, which caused them great suffering. The old, weak, and fractious were left behind in places, thus populating the route.

When the migration narrative carries the Mexica to Coatepec, Hill of the Serpent (*Coatl* = serpent, *tepetl* = hill), the story pauses for a digressive episode that reaches even deeper back into the mythical past to bring a past event into the narrative present. This episode concerns the birth of the Mexica god Huitzilopochtli. The legend, as it was written down by Bernardino de Sahagún, is that one day at Coatepec the old goddess Coatlicue (Serpents Her Skirt) was sweeping. "And once when Coatl icue was sweeping, feathers descended upon her—what was like a ball of feathers. Then Coatl icue snatched them up; she placed them at her waist. And when she had finished sweeping, then she would have taken the feathers which she had put at her waist. She found nothing.

According to legend, the priestess Coatlicue was magically impregnated by a ball of feathers that fell from the sky. This outraged her other children, who, at the urging of her grown daughter, Coyolxauhqui, planned to kill her. The unborn child, Huitzilopochtli, learned of this plot and was able to emerge wondrously from the womb as a fully armed and invincible warrior. Here Father Sahagún's artist paints Huitzilopochtli emerging beneath Coatlicue's skirt of intertwined serpents; the goddess' name means Serpents Her Skirt.

The legendary point of origin of many Nahuatl-speakers was the place of Seven Caves, known as Chicomoztoc, which appears at right in an illustration from the *Historia Tolteca-Chichimeca*. Different tribes wait in the seven cavities as a priest strikes the entrance with his staff. Footprints mark passage in and out of the cave; scrolls spewing from the mouths of individuals signify speech.

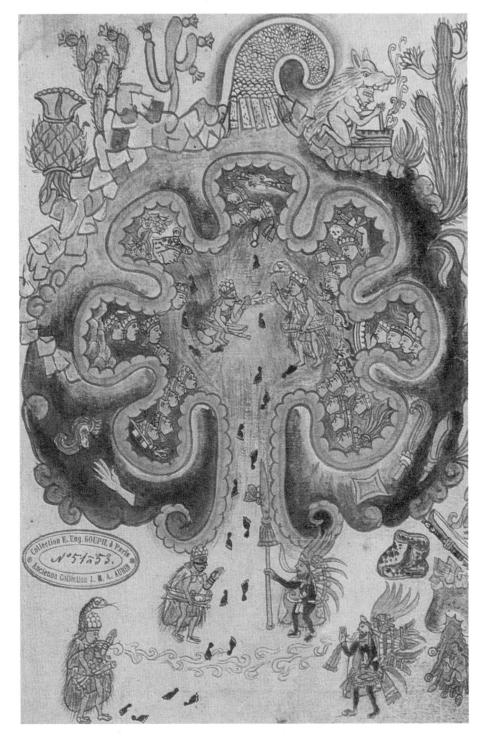

Thereupon by means of them Coatl icue conceived." As the child grew in her womb, her grown daughter, the goddess Coyolxauhqui (Painted with Bells) was shocked and horrified at her mother's sexual transgression. Coyolxauhqui plotted with her 400 brothers, the Centzon Huitznahua (400 being the equivalent of our 1001, meaning innumerable), to kill Coatlicue before she could give birth. To them Coyolxauhqui said, "My elder brothers, she hath dishonored us. We [can] only kill our mother, the wicked one who is already with child. Who is the cause of what is in her womb?" Huitzilopochtli, the unborn child, learned of this plot; at just the right moment, he burst forth fully grown and fully armed as a great warrior. "He pierced Coyolxauhqui, and then quickly struck off her head. It stopped there at the edge of Coatepetl [Coatepec]. And her body came falling below; it fell breaking to pieces; in various places her arms, her legs, her body each fell. And Uitzilopochtli then arose; he pursued, gave full attention to the Centzonuitznaua; he plunged, he scattered them from the top of Coatepetl."

After his dramatic birth, Huitzilopochtli brandished a fire-serpent weapon and conquered all who stood in his way. While his mother, Coatlicue, symbolized the earth, he came to represent the sun. As such, he emerged victorious each day, having vanquished his disloyal siblings, who became the stars.

Thus Huitzilopochtli slew Coyolxauhqui and her 400 brothers, decapitated them, dismembered them, and threw their bodies down the hill of Coatepec. Thereafter, Coyolxauhqui rose to become the moon, and the 400 Huitznahua rose to become the stars. Metaphorically, Huitzilopochtli is the sun; each day when he rises in the east he vanquishes the moon and the stars. The story was to become an important part of the Mexica rhetoric of victory, for the defeated Coyolxauhqui would later become a symbol for all of Huitzilopochtli's enemies.

After Huitzilopochtli's victory, the migration story resumes its narration of the Mexica's long journey. Gradually and circuitously, the impoverished band approached the Valley of Mexico. There they quickly discovered that all the prime lands were already occupied by settled peoples who had farmed these lands for centuries and who had migrated earlier. Despised as ruffians, the Mexica were forced to move from place to place, until they finally stopped at the hill on the western edge of Lake Texcoco called Chapultepec (Grasshopper Hill). Even here they were not safe. Huitzilopochtli warned them that this was not their promised land and that they should prepare for war, for they were surrounded by peoples who showed them no friendliness. When the attack came, their ruler was captured, carried to Culhuacan (Place of Those with Ancestors), and sacrificed.

The Mexica put themselves at the mercy of the Culhua lord. His was an old, venerated lineage that reached back to the famed Toltecs, accomplished masters of a civilization now destroyed. They begged him to give them a place to live, and he told them they could live nearby at Tizapan, a mean wilderness occupied only by vipers and lizards. But the Mexica were grateful; rather than perish at Tizapan, they killed the poisonous snakes and reptiles and feasted on them. Indeed, the historian Diego Durán records that the Mexica "became so fond of them as food that they almost totally consumed the snakes in that place." The tenacity of the Mexica astonished the Culhua, who gained a fearful respect for their hardy neighbors, knowing them to be favored by their god. The two peoples lived as compatible neighbors for some time; gradually they intermarried.

Then Huitzilopochtli determined that the Mexica should leave that place; he devised a scenario that would ensure a timely and discordant departure. As Father Durán recounts it, Huitzilopochtli instructed his priests to ask the Culhua lord for his beloved daughter who would rule the Mexica as Huitzilopochtli's bride. Once she had arrived, the Mexica "took the young princess of Colhuacan [Culhuacan], heiress of that kingdom, and sacrificed her. Then they skinned her and dressed one of the youths in her skin, as their deity had willed. Then they went to the sovereign of Colhuacan and asked him to come adore his own daughter and sacrifice to her as a goddess... [The king] accepted the invitation, calling together the dignitaries of his kingdom.... With great confidence, [he] arose and went to the temple. He entered the chamber of the idol and began to perform many ceremonies.... As the room was dark he distinguished no one. Taking with his hand a brazier with fire, he threw incense into it fervently. This began to burn and the room lighted up

The wanderings of the Mexica led them through the Valley of Mexico until they finally settled on an island in the shallows of Lake Texcoco. The lake was fed by sweetwater from surrounding springs and rivers, enabling the Mexica to create fertile farmlands called *chinampas* in the marshlands. Broad causeways connected Tenochtitlan to the mainland. From this center, the Aztec empire came to embrace the surrounding lakeside city-states, as well as far-flung tributary states.

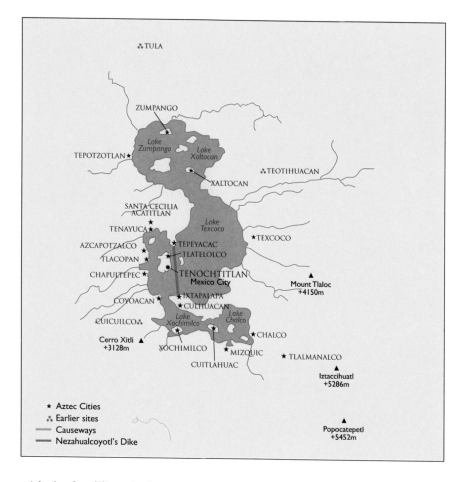

with the fire. Thus the king suddenly perceived the priest who was seated next to the idol, dressed in his daughter's skin. This was such a frightful sight that the king was filled with a wild terror. He dropped the brazier and rushed out of the temple shouting: 'Come here, come, O my vassals of Colhuacan! Come avenge the foul deed committed by the Aztecs! They have killed my daughter and dressed a youth in her skin and have made me worship him. Death and destruction to men so evil and with such vile customs! Let not a trace of their memory remain! Let us put an end to them!'" Whereupon the Mexica, just barely escaping with their lives, were evicted from Tizapan and driven deep into the reeds and marshes of the lake.

There they wandered in misery from place to place. Huitzilopochtli, seeing the despair and weeping of his people, promised to end their torment and lead them to their promised land.

As their god foretold, in the middle of the lake they came upon a prickly pear cactus growing from a stone, a cactus so wondrously tall and thick that a fine eagle nested in it. There they spotted the eagle, its wings outstretched in

The last and most miserable phase of the Mexica's migration ended when they came across a prickly pear cactus growing from a stone in the middle of Lake Texcoco. The plant was so lush that a great eagle was nesting in it, a sign to the weary travelers that they had found their promised land. They immediately set about founding their city. Subsequently, the symbol of the eagle and the cactus became the national emblem of the Republic of Mexico.

the morning sun. Father Durán records that in its talons the eagle held a shining bird; other versions of the story say the eagle held a mighty serpent. This image of the handsome eagle perched on the prickly pear cactus and grasping a writhing serpent has since become the national symbol for Mexico, just as it was the icon for Mexico-Tenochtitlan and the Aztec empire.

At last, at Tenochtitlan (Place of the Prickly Pear Cactus), the Mexica founded their new home. There, Huitzilopochtli foretold, they would find rest and grandeur; there, their name would be praised and their nation made great. They would rule over peoples near and distant, and would make Tenochtitlan a city to be queen over all others.

The Mexica migration story has all the elements of a transformational passage, whereby the Mexica are changed from their previous selves and are endowed with the characteristics necessary for their imperial success. They begin as Chichimecs, semi-barbarian people who exist by hunting, gathering, and occasionally employing agriculture, and emerge as suitable adversaries and allies to the powerful peoples in the valley. Aztlan, a fertile island that lies among reeds and grasses in a marshy lake, is recreated as Tenochtitlan. Along the route to this new Aztlan, their god Huitzilopochtli is born as an invincible warrior who destroys and scatters all his enemies; by this, the Mexica gain a fearsome warrior god. The many hardships along the migration give them strength and endurance. At Tizapan, for instance, they turn misfortune into a feast of serpent meat. By inter-marrying with the people from Culhuacan, they acquire venerable ancestors and link themselves to the ancient Toltecs. Then, when they sacrifice the Culhua lord's daughter they accomplish two things: First, they prove their unquestioning obedience to the ruthless Huitzilopochtli. Second, they separate themselves from the Culhua, under whom they had been serving as vassals, and are forced to found an independent capital. The migration has given them the three things they need for later imperial success: solidarity as an aggressive warrior people, Toltec ancestors, and autonomy in the Valley of Mexico.

All the other peoples in and around the valley had migration stories, too. Most of these peoples were Nahuatl-speakers who had preceeded the Mexica down from the arid northwest; they, also, were Chichimecs who became civi-lized. Their migration histories, like the Mexica's, charted their movement in a general way and indicated by which rights they came to control the territory they occupied. The stories differed in their particulars, but all were certain to mention that their people emerged from the caves of Chicomoztoc to endure a great period of moving from place to place. All the stories linked their people to the earlier Toltec civilization, either by explaining how the people migrated from the Toltec capital after its fall or by telling how they married into the Culhua dynasty, which was of Toltec ancestry. Then they told how their peo-ple defeated their enemies and founded their city. All these components seem to have been necessary for sovereign status.

The Acolhua, for example, who later became good allies of the Mexica, emerged from Chicomoztoc and were subsequently led into the Valley of Mexico by the Chichimec hero Xolotl; this happened long before the Mexica arrived. Their story is told by pictorial documents once in the Texcocan royal archive, and by the writings of Fernando de Alva Ixtlilxochitl, a descendant of Xolotl who translated the pictorial accounts nearly a century after the Spanish Conquest. These histories tell how Xolotl and his followers first came to the valley and established their base at the old Toltec stronghold of Tenayuca. Xolotl's son, who married a Culhua princess, and his grandson consolidated the Acolhua domain through conquests, alliances, and marriages. His great-grandson then moved from Tenayuca and established the autonomous Acolhua capital at Texcoco on the eastern shore of Lake Texcoco.

Migration stories such as these speak about a major movement of Nahuatl-speaking people coming down from the arid areas of northern Mexico and into the central valleys. This seems to have been the case in the several centuries after A.D. 800. Peoples on the northern edge of Mesoamerica had always been at the mercy of climatic change. During long periods when rain was relatively plentiful, great expanses of territory north of the central valleys could be and were cultivated. Such was the situation during the Toltec period (900-1150), when Mesoamerican culture extended far northward. But then drier conditions made much of this land inhospitable except to hunters and gatherers. The marginal peoples, the Chichimecs, who combined hunting, gathering, and agriculture, were driven down into the wetter valleys where their arrival put pressures on the settled peoples already there. Gradually, they adopted the cultural practices of the settled peoples and integrated with them, but their stories reveal that they wanted to preserve the memory of their Chichimec roots.

THE RECORD FROM THE LAND

Although the Mexica were newcomers to the Valley of Mexico, other peoples had been living and prospering there for thousands of years. The surviving documents do not feature these early people, however. We know about them principally through the archaeological record.

At 7000 feet (2134 meters) above sea level and ringed by high mountain chains, the Valley of Mexico offered a rich ecosystem for human life. Fertile lands surrounded the great system of shallow lakes: the large but brackish Lake Texcoco, fed by sweetwater lakes on the north (Xaltocan and Zumpango) and south (Xochimilco and Chalco). The marshy edges attracted wild birds, while the wooded slopes of the hillsides were home to deer and turkey. Some 7500 years before the birth of Christ, humans were hunting imperial mammoths along the lake shore. The archaeological record tells us that the hunters butchered the great beasts in the muddy flats that trapped them, and left stone projectile points and knives among the carcasses.

Later peoples cultivated crops of corn, cotton, and other plants at various places along the lake. From Pre-Classic sites like Tlatilco, where brickworkers digging for clay in the 1940s found an ancient cemetery, archaeologists have uncovered modeled ceramic figurines and vessels dating from between 1500 and 900 B.C. Some of the 500 graves at Tlatilco contained exquisitely worked whole vessels, enchanting figurines, masks, and ornaments, many in the local style but others in styles more characteristic of the Gulf Coast, Morelos, and distant Oaxaca. The stylistic mix tells us that this farming community, like others in the area, was already tied into an extensive network of trade or travel, the same network that spread Gulf Coast Olmec elements across Mesoamerica.

By 400 B.C., the valley population had increased greatly. Two sites began to emerge as the dominant polities in their different areas of the basin: Teotihuacan in the northeast, and Cuicuilco in the southwest.

At Cuicuilco, just west of Lake Xochimilco, the inhabitants constructed a massive civic-ceremonial structure; piling adobes almost 90 feet (27 meters) high, they formed a broad circular temple platform, then faced it with stones to a diameter of

The circular pyramid at Cuicuilco is all that remains of what was once a leading city in the Valley of Mexico, with a population of more than 20,000. Until around 100 B.C., Cuicuilco competed with Teotihuacan for land and resources. Its florescence was cut short, however, when the nearby volcano Xitli erupted. A later eruption buried the area in molten lava.

260 feet (80 meters). With an estimated population of more than 20,000, Cuicuilco competed aggressively with Teotihuacan for land and resources, but not for long. Shortly before 100 B.C. the nearby volcano Xitli erupted and effectively destroyed Cuicuilco as a power; the molten lava from a later eruption then flowed over the site, covering much of the pyramid, and transforming the countryside of the southwestern valley into a volcanic desert (now called the Pedregal).

The destruction of Cuicuilco left Teotihuacan as the only major center in the basin and the magnet for its people. As the population of Teotihuacan began to swell in the first centuries A.D., its visionary architects laid plans for a grandiose ceremonial precinct, one without parallel in Mesoamerica. Over a sacred cave, in a single work effort, they constructed an enormous stepped pyramid, now called the Pyramid of the Sun. Faced with cut stone, the pyramid stood some 200 feet (more than 60 meters) high. One still sees it from many miles away, rising steeply above the Teotihuacan valley floor.

At this time, too, they laid out the controlling axis of the site, a broad way called by the Aztecs the Street of the Dead, running from the so-called Pyramid of the Moon complex at the north, past the Pyramid of the Sun, and down to a vast wide courtyard, the Ciudadela (or Citadel), which became the political center of the city later in its history. In the Ciudadela, Teotihuacan authorities sacrificed more than 200 individuals, burying them in mass graves prior to building the Temple of the Feathered Serpent over them. Altars, shrines, and temples lined the Street of the Dead; the grandest palaces were built along it to house the city's elite. The ceremonial center of Teotihuacan became the most impressive ritual arena ever constructed in Mesoamerica; only the giant pyramid then being built at Cholula across the mountains would rival it.

The rest of the city of Teotihuacan was as grand as its ceremonial core. From throughout the basin of Mexico and even from across the mountains

At its height, around A.D. 600, the city of Teotihuacan covered almost 9 square miles (22.5 square kilometers) and was home to between 125,000 and 200,000 people. Today, the Pyramid of the Sun and the long ritual way known as the Street of the Dead bear testament to the city's past glory and the religious life of its inhabitants.

in Tlaxcala, people poured into the urban center, which grew proportionally. At its height, around A.D. 600, the city covered almost 9 square miles (22.5 square kilometers) and housed somewhere between 125,000 and 200,000 people. A grid pattern organized the city's building program into four quarters. Distinct neighborhoods, like the Oaxaca *barrio*, became the locus of foreigners residing in the city. Thousands of apartment compounds, each housing between 60 and 100 people, crowded families together.

The cosmopolitan center bustled with commercial and religious activities. A key to its vast mercantile strength was its monopoly of the obsidian trade. Obsidian was the cutting tool of choice throughout Mesoamerica, and Teotihuacan controlled its production and distribution. The city had strong commercial and political ties with the Gulf Coast, Oaxaca, the Maya region, and the northwest.

The dominance of Teotihuacan went unchallenged until around A.D. 750. Then, according to archaeologist René Millon, a series of calamitous fires broke out and destroyed the religious and political nucleus of the city. The archaeological evidence indicates that the fires were intentionally set; moreover, sculptures were toppled and monuments smashed in a frenzy of destruction. It is not certain whether the culprits were a foreign force or an unhappy local population pushed to the limits, because most of the city was left largely undisturbed. Even after Teotihuacan's once-majestic heart had been gutted, some 30,000 to 50,000 people continued to live in the city for generations.

Hundreds of years after Teotihuacan's power had waned, its architectural grandeur still inspired those who visited its ruins. The built city of Teotihuacan was the prototype in Mesoamerica for a densely packed urban center. Its monumental ceremonial precinct and its regular grid system became general models for the layout of Tenochtitlan.

The Aztecs wrapped the city in legend. They gave it its present name, Teotihuacan, which means Place of the Gods; they believed the pyramids to be the tombs of ancient monarchs who had become divine. Finding mammoth bones from the late Paleolithic period nearby, they thought Teotihuacan itself had been built by giants. There in the Ciudadela, the Aztecs believed, the gods created the world; there the gods had gathered to create the sun and the moon and set them in motion. And there, at Teotihuacan, the emperor Moctezuma used to go regularly to perform rituals and make sacrifices.

The Aztecs also venerated the city that was to follow Teotihuacan as the mightiest power in Mesoamerica. That city was Tula (the ancient Tollan), capital of the Toltecs.

In the wake of Teotihuacan's decline, semi-nomadic Nahuatl-speakers came down from the north, much like the Aztecs would do later. These Toltecs settled in Culhuacan in the Valley of Mexico, but eventually located their capital at Tula about 50 miles (80 kilometers) north. The site, at the northern edge of reliable agricultural lands, took advantage of nearby rivers that gave access both to the Gulf Coast and to west Mexico, with which the Toltecs developed strong ties. Tula was never as big as Teotihuacan; still, it grew to a sizable city of 30,000 to 60,000 people and may well have been the largest city in Mesoamerica at the time. From this capital, the

The central element of this ceramic brazier found at Teotihuacan is a human face richly adorned with large ear-spools and a complex feather headdress. Added elements point to a deity or cult of the butterfly; the plume resembles a stylized butterfly proboscis.

41

Toltecs established an empire, based upon military coercion, which dominated Central Mexico from 900 to 1150.

The Aztecs looked to the Toltecs as an imperial prototype. At Tula, the architectural and sculptural program spoke clearly of militaristic power dominating by force. The principal temple-pyramid at the site, now called Pyramid B, was faced with stone relief carvings of eagles, jaguars, coyotes, and pumas—all savage carnivores that may have represented the warrior orders. Great stone warriors, more than 11 feet (3.5 meters) in height, supported the roof of the temple; stone serpents supported the doorway. A colonnaded portico linked the temple with the large colonnaded halls next door. There, relief carvings of long files of warriors led to a central altar, carved with a scene of bloodletting. All of these architectural and sculptural features the Aztecs eagerly adopted for their own imperial structures, just as they imitated the Toltec chacmools (altars carved in the shape of seated/reclining warriors). Indeed, the Aztecs did more than copy Toltec artworks; long after the fall of Tula, the Aztecs looted the ceremonial center and carried off many sculptures to erect them in their own capital.

To the people who followed, the Toltecs were a glorious race. According to Aztec stories recorded by Father Sahagún and others, the Toltec patron deity had given them knowledge, so that they were masters of wisdom; they were learned; they were skilled artists and craftspersons, who invented turquoise and feather mosaic. They were great healers, who invented the art of medicine; they excelled at agriculture, growing cotton in many colors and harvesting abundant crops. They were devout, righteous, and rich. As Sahagún sums it up: "The Tolteca were wise. Their works were all good, all perfect, all wonderful, all marvelous; their houses beautiful...." The word Tolteca became synonymous with skilled artist. It is no wonder the Aztecs determined to marry into this line of heroes and take up the Toltecs as their ancestors.

When Tula fell, around A.D. 1150-1200, it may have been because internal dissent had undercut the political structure; a wave of Chichimecs moving down out of an increasingly arid north may have struck the final blow. Aztec legends about Tula's downfall tell how the ruler Quetzalcoatl (Feathered Serpent) fled the city with his followers, moving eastward to the Gulf of Mexico. One version of the story describes how, there on the shore, Quetzalcoatl set himself on fire to become Venus the Morning Star; another version has him setting sail on a raft of serpents and vowing to return in the year 1 Reed (the year of his birth).

The vacuum left by the demise of Tula was partially filled by a scattering of growing polities. Some, like Culhuacan, had lingering Toltec affiliations; indeed, Culhuacan remained important as the last seat of the Toltec dynasty. Other communities were founded by the incoming Chichimecs, who gradually intermarried with the local peoples and took on the mantle of civilization. The Acolhua established themselves at Tenayuca on the western edge of the lake and then moved the seat of their power across the lake to Texcoco. The Tepanecs

Pyramid B, also called the Pyramid of the Morning Star, was the heart of the Toltec capital of Tula. Despite the city's disintegration in the 12th century A.D., Toltec civilization became a model and object of veneration for the Aztecs. Standing guard atop the pyramid are four massive statues of warriors carved in basalt, as well as the remains of serpent columns and carved pillars. All of these originally helped to support the roof of the temple. The warrior columns, one of which is shown below, are known as Atlantean statues. One of the four at the site is a reconstruction; the original is now housed in Mexico City's National Museum of Anthropology.

dominated the western side of the lake from their city of Azcapotzalco, named the Place of the Ant Hill because it was so heavily populated. In the south, the Chalca and the Xochimilca controlled the rich agricultural lands. It was into this mix of peoples that the Mexica ventured during the final years of their migration.

The story of the peoples who prospered and declined in the Valley of Mexico draws intermittently on the documentary and the archaeological records. Written and painted histories are silent about the first humans who walked the land, about the early farming communities, and about the towns and cities that followed them; these documents give us only the barest glimpse of Teotihuacan. We therefore rely on the archaeological record to put together the broad outlines of their stories, which necessarily remain incomplete and impersonal. Excavation and analysis of the material remains at Tlatilco may not identify the community's rulers and gods, but they do tell us about some of its connections with the rest of Mesoamerica. Archaeology reveals the awesome sacrifice of 200 individuals, most dressed as warriors, just before a temple pyramid was constructed at Teotihuacan, but it does not yet tell us why these individuals were chosen to die that way, or who they were.

As we approach the Aztec period itself, the written records are more abundant and fulsome, but the archaeology is murkier because most of the principal Aztec sites in the valley have always been occupied. Modern Mexico City overlies Tenochtitlan, just as modern Texcoco sits over the Acolhua capital. Few excavators have had permission to scour away present-day businesses and residences to get at the early-16th-century ruins beneath. The ethnohistorical sources become increasingly important, therefore, both for the overview they can give of Aztec culture, and for the names and motivations of the individuals who lived it.

The bravery and skill in combat of Aztec warriors, some of whom are depicted here in a detail from the *Codex Mendoza*, was legendary. The As the leading member of the so-called Triple Alliance, which included Tenochtitlan, Texcoco, and Tlacopan, the Mexica rapidly established

Aztec culture of war helped to forge an empire.
military superiority over their rivals.

3
THE IMPERIAL STORY

By noting the omens and obeying the directions of their god, the Mexica finally came to the place of their destiny in the year 1 Flint (1324)—the year sign for great beginnings. The next year, the first full year of their residence, was also appropriate to the task before them, because that year—2 House—was auspicious for settling down. (The painted and textual histories prefer it as the year of Tenochtitlan's founding.) Bolstered by the fine prognostications of these year signs, the Mexica began the work of building Tenochtitlan. They immediately erected a simple shrine for Huitzilopochtli. They then spent long days laboring hard to shore up the swampy edges of their island, firm the land, and build houses of wood and thatch. Between pilings driven into the shallow lake bed, they piled up rich muddy soil to create fertile agricultural plots raised just above the water's edge. These raised beds, called *chinampas*, would always demand much tending, but the Mexica knew they were the source of their neighbors' abundant crops. Following the instructions of Huitzilopochtli, they divided their city into four main wards, or districts, which radiated out from Huitzilopochtli's central precinct. During these early years, one faction of the people left Tenochtitlan to found a sister city, Tlatelolco, on the next island to the north.

The most powerful people in the valley were the Tepanecs, led by the tough and wily ruler Tezozomoc, whose capital city, Azcapotzalco, lay nearby on the western lakeshore. The struggling Aztecs survived in their early years as Tepanec vassals, paying a stiff tribute and serving as mercenaries while Tezozomoc expanded his domain. Fighting alongside the Tepanec army, the Mexica warriors honed their combat skills and gained an increased reputation for bravery.

When it came time to establish their royal dynasty, the Mexica looked to Culhuacan, that seat of Toltec bloodlines with whom the Mexica had lived and intermarried years before. Wisely, they did not mention their earlier ill-treatment of a Culhua princess. The stories tell how the Mexica went before the Culhua lord, saying "we must have a ruler to guide us and show us how we are to live, who will free us and protect us from our enemies." They asked that he give them Acamapichtli (Handful of Arrows), the son of a Mexica noble-man and the Culhua ruler's daughter. Pleased to grant their request, the Culhua lord replied, "Let Acamapichtli rule over the waters and the lands of the Aztec people. But I warn you that if my grandson were a woman I would not give her to you." In the propitious year 1 Flint (1376), a 52-year cycle after their arrival at the Place of the Prickly Pear Cactus, Acamapichtli became the first Mexica *tlatoani*, literally "speaker." He took as his wife a woman of Culhua royalty, adding even more Toltec blood to the Mexica line. It was this strong mix of Toltec and Mexica that the Mexica celebrated when they referred to themselves as the Culhua-Mexica.

Acamapichtli and his successors—his son Huitzilihuitl (Hummingbird Feather) and grandson Chimalpopoca (Smoking Shield)—solidified the Mexica's position in the valley in the next 50 years. They guided the early construction of the city, accomplished a number of local conquests on their own, and chose wives wisely. Huitzilihuitl married the daughter of their Tepanec overlord Tezozomoc, who subsequently became so fond of his grandson Chimalpopoca that he lightened the Mexica's tribute burden to a mere token of ducks, fish, and frogs. The Mexica had become more like allies than vassals. It was during this time that Tezozomoc tried to absorb the polity of Texcoco across the lake, a feat he nearly accomplished by killing the Texcocan ruler and

TENOCHTITLAN'S ROYAL DYNASTY

The royal dynasty of Tenochtitlan began with Acamapichtli (Handful of Arrows), who was the son of a Mexica lord and a Culhua princess and thus had Toltec blood running through his veins. Succession to the office of *huey tlatoani*, or "great speaker," stayed with the royal family but could pass from brother to brother, from uncle to nephew, and from grandfather to grandson, depending on individual merit. When Moctezuma Xocoyotzin, or Moctezuma the Younger, died during the Spanish Conquest, his brother Cuitlahuac ruled until he died 80 days later of smallpox; then, to continue the resistance, their cousin Cuauhtemoc was elected ruler.

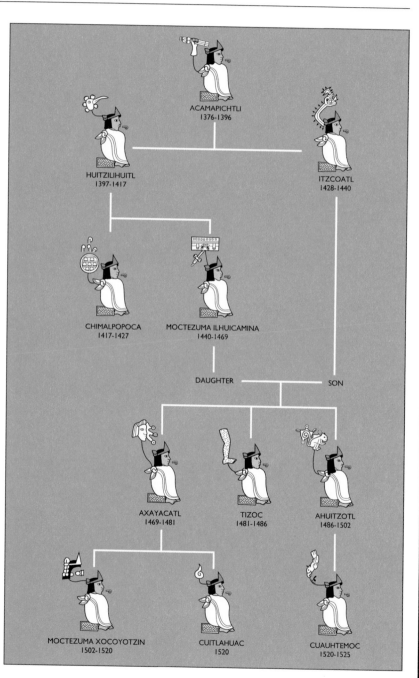

An eagle perched atop a nopal cactus marks the site of Tenochtitlan's founding in this painting from the *Codex Mendoza.* Wavy blue bands framing and cutting across the island represent the surrounding lake and the canals that divide the island into four quarters. The leaders of the tribe's clan groups, shown seated, wear their hair drawn up in warriors' topknots and have their name glyphs attached to them by a line. The shield and arrows below Tenochtitlan's place glyph signify the warfare that will bring the Mexica greatness. At the bottom, the Mexica celebrate victories over the rival cities of Culhuacan and Tenayuca.

forcing the son into exile. The son, Nezahualcoyotl (Hungry Coyote), was a relative of the Mexica rulers and would soon become their loyal ally.

The cozy relationship between the Mexica and Tepanecs changed as Tepanec factions increasingly came to resent the Mexica's favored status and their arrogance. When Tezozomoc died an old man, his successor murdered Chimalpopoca and the lord of nearby Tlatelolco, and increased the Mexica's tribute payments. This aggression was the last straw. Shortly after taking office, Chimalpopoca's uncle, Itzcoatl (Obsidian Serpent), formed a coalition with other lakeside peoples against the Tepanecs. Allying himself with the exiled Nezahualcoyotl of Texcoco (his nephew) and relying on the help of the people of Tlacopan, Itzcoatl and his forces defeated the Tepanecs after a hard-fought battle and sacked the city of Azcapotzalco, bringing an end to Tepanec domination of the basin of Mexico.

In its place came the Triple Alliance, a coalition of Tenochtitlan, Texcoco, and Tlacopan for joint control of Mexico. Armies from the three polities were to participate together in conquests, and the cities would share in the incoming tribute. Several of the chroniclers mention a tribute ratio of two-fifths each for Tenochtitlan and Texcoco and one-fifth for Tlacopan, but most accounts suggest that Tenochtitlan soon outshone its weaker allies and assumed control. The Aztec annals and chronicles speak of Itzcoatl as the founder of the empire. It should come as no surprise to us that they also say he acceded to office in the propitious year 1 Flint (1428).

Itzcoatl followed his young nephew Chimalpopoca as tlatoani, or ruler. Aztec inheritance tended to go first from brother to brother, and then to the eldest son of the eldest brother, but succession to the tlatoani throne followed no set pattern. More important was that a new ruler have the dual virtues of elegant speech and bravery on the battlefield, for he would be called upon to be an effective diplomat for his people and to lead his armies into battle if diplomacy should fail. Additionally, the tlatoani was the living incarnation of their god Huitzilopochtli. A council of elders selected Itzcoatl, like the three *tlatoque* (plural of tlatoani) before him, as the most meritorious of those eligible members of the royal family. Father Durán notes that Itzcoatl "was elected king by common accord" because he was "so courageous, a man of such excellent life, that he outshone all of his brothers." It was a wise choice. After defeating Azcapotzalco, Itzcoatl soon launched a military sweep that brought most of the remaining polities in the Valley of Mexico under Aztec control. His crucial conquest of the rich chinampa cities in the south (Xochimilco, Cuitlahuac, Mizquic) added long-sought fertile farmlands.

If Itzcoatl established the fact of the Aztec empire and its dominion over the Valley of Mexico, his successor, Moctezuma Ilhuicamina, gave it range. Moctezuma Ilhuicamina (Angry Lord, Archer in the Sky), also called Moctezuma the Elder, had already distinguished himself as a brilliant military leader under Itzcoatl. During his long reign (1440-1469), he established the Aztecs' victorious military program. His armies successfully carried Aztec control

49

southward into Morelos, westward into Guerrero, and eastward through Puebla and southern Veracruz; he stretched the young empire from ocean to ocean.

At home, Moctezuma sought to make Tenochtitlan a fitting capital. Workers renovated and enlarged the temple complex to Huitzilopochtli. They built a new aqueduct to bring sweet water from Chapultepec to the city's heart. In collaboration with his kinsman Nezahualcoyotl, the poet king of Texcoco, Moctezuma also built a great dike to separate the brackish waters of the eastern lake from the sweeter waters around Tenochtitlan and the chinampa cities to its south.

In the year 1454, a great drought came and lingered for three years over the central valleys. The alphabetic histories record how "the springs dried up, the streams and rivers ceased to run, the earth burned like fire and, from sheer dryness, cracked in great clefts.... As soon as maize sprouted it turned yellow and withered like all the rest of the crops." The people suffered and starved; many abandoned their homes to depart for more fertile lands. After all the storehouses were empty, the people sold themselves and their children into slavery, saying "we will sell our sons and daughters to those who can feed them so that they do not starve to death." Painted annals picture how the new slaves lined up one behind the other, yoked around their necks, to be led from the city. "They went along weeping and their wails reached the heavens." Many went to the land of the Totonacs along the Gulf Coast in Veracruz, where harvests were abundant. It was known as the drought and famine of the year 1 Rabbit. It added impetus to Moctezuma's campaign to bring the fertile lands of the Gulf Coast under his control.

Axayacatl (Water Face), the sixth tlatoani, took up Moctezuma's program of outward expansion after his grandfather's death. Under the young ruler, the empire grew into new territories along the Gulf Coast; westward it expanded into the Toluca Valley and Matlatzinca country. Closer inward there were sporadic rebellions to suppress. When animosity developed with Tlatelolco, Tenochtitlan's neighbor and ally, Axayacatl conquered and subjected the market city. Axayacatl's string of victories came to an end, however. On the northwest edge of the empire, the Aztec forces met with a disastrous defeat at the hands of the wild and fierce Tarascans of Michoacan. The Tarascans never did submit to Aztec dominion.

Axayacatl's unhappy loss presaged a brief period when the Aztec military machine seem to have stalled. Axayacatl's successor and brother, Tizoc (Chalk Leg), is portrayed by later Aztec historians as having been relatively weak and cowardly in battle. As Durán's Nahuatl history sums it up: "his life was short and his deeds few." Tizoc ruled only five years (1481-1486), his principal achievement being to initiate a major renovation and expansion of the Templo Mayor complex. It was said that members of his court poisoned him.

The third brother to take the throne, Ahuitzotl (Water Beast), shared none of Tizoc's weaknesses or vacillations. Ahuitzotl was a young man still in the school for noble youths when he became tlatoani, yet he rivaled his grandfather

Moctezuma in expanding the empire. Under him, the Aztec world extended from coast to coast, from the Huasteca in northern Veracruz to the Isthmus of Tehuantepec in the southeast, and reaching up the Pacific shores of Guerrero north of Acapulco to the Balsas drainage. War prisoners brought back to Tenochtitlan from his successful campaigns in the south gave their lives to dedicate his greatest achievement: this was the newly renovated Templo Mayor, begun under Tizoc but completed in all its glory by Ahuitzotl in the year 8 Reed (1487).

The Aztecs had enlarged the religious complex dedicated to Huitzilopochtli and the rain god Tlaloc many times over the years, but this renovation under Ahuitzotl was almost inconceivably grand. Masons, plasterers, and painters labored to finish the structures, and sculptors furiously carved images of the gods and goddesses and all the other elements of the new sculptural program. Planning a sumptuous feast and an awe-inspiring display for its dedication, Ahuitzotl invited all his vassals to bring victims for sacrifice. He ordered a cessation of hostilities so that his adversaries from Tlaxcala, Huejotzingo, and Cholula could attend. The day of the solemn sacrifice, the chroniclers describe how long lines of victims whose hearts were to be torn out stretched beyond the edges of the city and down the wide causeways. The painted history of the *Codex Telleriano-Remensis* numbers the victims at 20,000, and some other estimates are four times that high. Later the guests, friend and foe alike, "departed from Mexico bewildered by the majesty of the city and the amazing number of victims who had died."

The shining accomplishments of Ahuitzotl's successor, Moctezuma Xocoyotzin (Angry Lord, The Younger), tend to be dimmed by his humiliation at the hands of the Spanish. Historians trying to explain the Conquest have considered him indecisive and weak, but he was not so before the Spanish arrived to interpret his actions differently. The Nahuatl history translated by Father Durán characterizes Moctezuma as "a mature man, pious, virtuous, generous and of an invincible spirit. He was blessed with all the virtues that can be found in a good ruler and his decisions had always been correct, especially in matters of war. In the latter he had performed feats which showed remarkable bravery." Moctezuma pursued successful military campaigns in Oaxaca, taking over rich Mixtec holdings, and he gained important footholds in the Maya area by adding Chiapas and Xoconosco to the Aztec domain. Following a policy of consolidation, he waged hard wars against Tlaxcala and Huejotzingo. By the time the Spanish arrived in 1519, Moctezuma and his predecessors had left few independent territories: Tlaxcala and its neighbors in Huejotzingo and

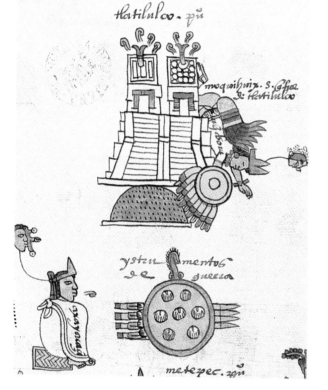

The historical section of the *Codex Mendoza* lists the rulers of Tenochtitlan and itemizes their conquests. This detail depicts Axacayatl, shown lower left, and identified by his name glyph (Water Face), speech scroll, and royal crown. Pictured, too, is his conquest of Tlatelolco, including the dramatic death of its ruler.

Cholula; the small Meztitlan enclave in the north; the rough terrain of the barbarous Yopes in Guerrero; and the principality of Tototepec in southern Oaxaca. On the outer edges of the empire, the Tarascans and the Maya remained beyond Aztec control, the Tarascans being too fierce and the Maya being too distant and dispersed to be of much interest.

CULTURE OF WAR

The force that created this vast empire was a culture of war. From the first days of their lives, Aztec children were prepared for their roles as courageous warriors. The boys might eventually gain glory on the battlefield, where their umbilical cords were taken and buried soon after the boys were born. The girls could one day achieve victory by giving birth. New rulers had to gain victory in battle before they could fully assume office. Huitzilopochtli, the warrior god, demanded the hearts of captives taken in battle.

Metaphors of war pervaded Aztec thought. The warriors were the eagles, the jaguars. The sun, too, was a warrior, an ascending eagle who daily fought its way across the heavens. Those men who died on the battlefield or on the sacrificial stone after having been taken captive in battle were resurrected as butterflies; they accompanied the sun on its journey through the heavens from sunrise to noon. Thus, a new ruler's inaugural speech, recorded by Father Sahagún, exalts "the eagle warriors, the ocelot [jaguar] warriors, the valiant warriors, those who died in war, who rejoice, who are gladdened, who take pleasure, who live in abundance, who sip [the flower nectar] forever, who always cry out to [the sun], who gladden the sun, the valiant warrior...."

Childbirth was metaphorically a battle. An Aztec oration recorded by Sahagún tells us that a woman in labor had "become as an eagle warrior, ...as an ocelot warrior;" she "returned exhausted from battle." On the birth of a child, "the midwife shouted; she gave war cries, which meant that the little woman had fought a good battle, had become a brave warrior, had taken a captive, had captured a baby." Those brave women who died in childbirth became goddesses who rose heavenward to accompany the sun from noon to sunset. Armed as for war, these deified women "rose up; they came ascending to meet the noonday sun; ...there the eagle-ocelot warriors, those who had died in war, delivered the sun into the hands of the women...[who] carried it with a litter...gladdening it with war cries."

As a fundamental part of Aztec life, warfare was controlled by decorum and ceremony. No army (Aztec or foe) could rush brashly into battle without proper provocation and without following a series of prior negotiations, for war was universally understood to be ritualized conflict that followed a ritualized insult. Generally, the aggressor considered itself to have been insulted in some way; its merchants had been killed, or its politely worded request for goods or services had been denied. If the Aztecs wished to bring another city under their control, their envoys might repeatedly invite the foreign ruler to join the empire,

This terra-cotta sculpture of an eagle warrior, one of two found during the excavation of the Templo Mayor, stands roughly 6 feet (2 meters) in height. The figure marked the location of a meeting place for the Eagle and Jaguar Knights, the most important of the noble military orders. Originally, this guardian warrior was enlivened with plaster and paint, and held weapons in his hands.

pay tribute, and worship Huitzilopochtli; rebuffs, of course, were taken as insults. At this point, Aztec ambassadors would give formal notification of intent to do battle. They took gifts of arms—a shield and an obsidian-edged war club—to the enemy ruler as symbolic assurance that his forces would be well-equipped and prepared; they also brought him the feathered headdress worn by the dead to assure him of his impending defeat. No polity wanted to be accused of treachery. Finally the armies would meet at a predetermined location on a propitious day, and pray the gods favored them. After the battle, the winner and loser would renegotiate tribute arrangements. Warfare began and ended with fine negotiation and ceremony.

During Moctezuma the Elder's reign, for example, the conquest of nearby Chalco was sparked, so the chronicles say, by Chalco's repeated refusal to send stone for sculptures to adorn Huitzilopochtli's temple. After a few days of uneventful fighting, the Chalca asked their Mexica "brothers" to postpone the battle until the feast of their principal deity: "We wish to celebrate it with great solemnity and smear our temple with the blood of Aztecs so that our god will be the more glorified. Therefore, we ask that on that sacred day you join us in battle so that we may honor our god with your flesh." This the Mexica naturally did, believing in the superior strength of their own god and vowing to "make a great and solemn fire sacrifice with the bodies of men from Chalco."

The purpose of Aztec warfare was not to kill the enemy. No one desired the slaughter or eradication of a foe, regardless of what might be said in the inflammatory rhetoric before battle. Conquered cities were not usually pillaged either. One of the prime motivations for war was to conquer outside peoples and bring them into the empire. A stripped city and a destroyed people, however, would be of little worth, for they would be in no position to add much tribute to the empire's coffers. Instead, the Aztecs sought an honorable defeat for their enemies, after which they would ceremoniously burn their temple, install the worship of Huitzilopochtli, and bring the conquered people into the empire as contributing members.

The second motivation for war was to gain victims for the sacrificial stones. Warriors on all sides went into battle with the mission of taking prisoners, who would be brought home to be sacrificed to the captors' gods. Captives taken in battle were the marker for advancement in the warrior ranks. Fighters gained prestige according to the number of captives they took single-handedly. Kills on the battlefield did not count in the same way; one's foe had to be taken alive. The chronicles even specify that certain captives were better than others: prisoners taken from the well-trained Nahuatl-speaking armies of Tlaxcala and Huejotzingo carried the greatest prestige.

"Wars of Flowers," as they were called, were instituted in times of relative peace so that warriors on all sides could practice their skills and gain honor. Father Durán's history tells how Moctezuma the Elder challenged Huejotzingo, a long-term enemy, to a War of Flowers. "The men of Huexotzinco were delighted and accepted his challenge with good will." Moctezuma then invited anyone in the "allied kingdoms who wished to gain honor [to] present himself upon the plains near Atlixco within three days.... [Thereupon] one hundred thousand soldiers, the highest and most illustrious men of the three kingdoms, met upon the battlefield, all of them in splendid array. The Huexotzinca then appeared, no less finely attired and in equally good spirits, looking as if they had come to a festival."

This War of Flowers, like other battles, drew on a broad spectrum of Aztec society. Although there was no standing army as such, much of the population was pulled into service from time to time, either to fight or to feed, house, and

54

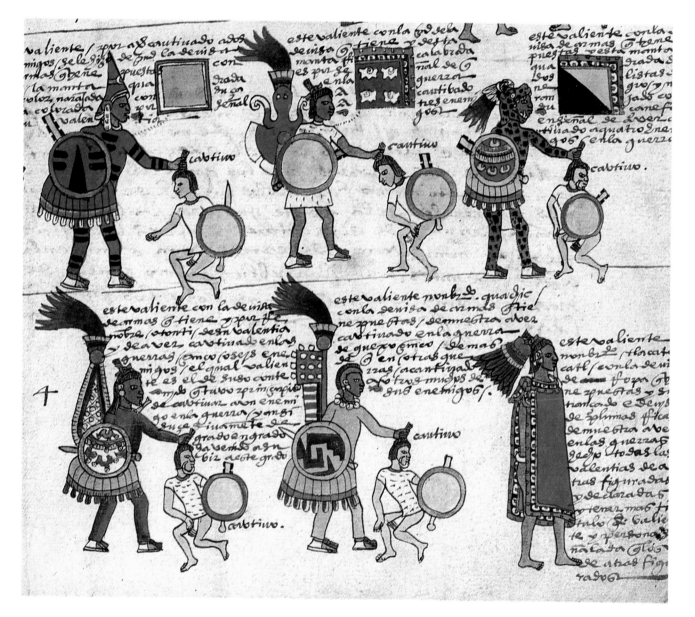

The rewards for taking prisoners in battle ranged from a red feather costume (*top left*) for two prisoners to a jaguar costume (*top right*) for taking four, as explained in the *Codex Mendoza*. The figure at the bottom right wears the feather decoration and mantle reserved for high military leaders.

assist the warriors. Most males had been prepared for battle since childhood. The *Codex Mendoza*, a pictorial record of Aztec victories, tribute, and daily life, shows how males could advance through the warrior ranks, taking prisoners and thereby gaining increased prestige. To the top of this human pyramid rose an elite group of fighting men, seasoned warriors who had distinguished themselves in battle. They had taken four or more prisoners and had been rewarded with lands and gifts by the emperor. They were organized into knightly orders, among which the Eagle Knights and the Jaguar Knights were the most prestigious.

55

On the battlefield, the warriors made a glorious sight. With each new captive taken, a man would gain the right to wear the distinctive costume appropriate to his rank. Plain shields and simple armor of quilted cotton protected the unproved fighters, but the distinguished veterans wore full-body suits brilliantly covered with brightly colored feathers; their shields, helmets, headdresses, and towering back devices were all embellished with luminous feathers and precious metals. They wielded deadly wooden swords edged in slivers of obsidian, and they fought to the sound of drums, trumpets, and pipes.

These elite warriors had become, in effect, professional soldiers who were supported in luxury by the empire. They included commoners as well as nobles. They formed a military meritocracy that increasingly drew on the empire's resources and tribute, thereby coming into competition with the nobility. From the warriors' headquarters, the Eagle House, next to the ruler's palace, the war council advised the ruler on military matters, including conquests and expansion.

THE IMPERIAL PATTERN

The empire created by this culture of war expanded with successive rulers until it reached much of civilized Mesoamerica. Aztec governors and tribute collectors walked the shores of both oceans, from Tampico to Tehuantepec, and the mountains and plains in between. Never a homogenous empire, it was composed of peoples who spoke different languages and had their own distinct customs. The relationship between each group, each province, and the imperial government varied also. There were tribute provinces and strategic provinces. The empire's livelihood depended on goods sent from the rich tribute provinces, but it was held together by the warriors and services provided by the strategic provinces.

Tribute was the raison d'être of imperial expansion. As is explained more thoroughly in Chapter 5, the Aztecs relied on tribute from distant and nearby peoples to feed the capital, and to maintain the nobility and the warrior knights. Luxury goods came from as far away as Guatemala, while grains arrived in great quantity from fertile lands closer to home and especially from the wealthy chinampa cities in the southern valley. The Aztecs drew peoples into the empire as tribute-paying provinces because they valued and needed the products of that region: exotic feathers and jaguar skins from Guatemala, gold from the mines of Guerrero, jewelry from Oaxaca, wood and cotton from Morelos, spondyllus shell from Colima. From such provinces, the wealth of the empire flowed into the capital, whence it was distributed out again either as favors and rewards by the emperor, or as trade goods to be exchanged for commodities beyond the empire's borders.

The Aztecs brought other peoples into the empire to protect the tribute provinces. Their territories were strategically important for the protection of the empire. These strategic provinces did not send tribute to the imperial capital. Instead they functioned as buffer zones on the edges or trouble spots of the empire. They provided armies when needed along the distant frontiers, and they often maintained garrisons of soldiers at the ready. When allied forces from the heartland marched to battle in these distant lands, the strategic provinces were there to provide the armies with food and supplies. Generally, the strategic provinces were located near rich tribute-paying provinces that lay on or near the frontiers of the empire, where the danger was greatest. When Axayacatl suffered his crushing defeat at the hands of the Tarascans in Michoacan, his allied forces from the Valley of Mexico were supported and reinforced by the Matlatzinca, who had only shortly before been brought into the empire.

Not every parcel of land or every territory was conquered by the Aztecs. There remained enclaves of hostile people who were never brought under Aztec control. In West Mexico, the wild Yopes eluded Aztec domination, as did the Otomi of Meztitlan in the north. The Mixtec kingdom of Tototepec in southern Oaxaca remained independent, although it probably would have fallen eventually. The greatest of the unconquered foes lived within the Aztec heartland, however. These were the Nahuatl-speaking peoples of Tlaxcala, Cholula, and Huejotzingo in the Tlaxcala and Puebla valleys, who culturally were like the Aztecs but who remained tenacious enemies who caused the Aztecs great woe.

Outside the empire there were enemies—the Tarascans, for instance, who had repulsed the Aztecs—but more often the foreign peoples had simply not yet been incorporated. They were still too distant and not sufficiently important for the great reach their conquest would require. Such was the case with the northern Maya of the Yucatan, with whom Aztec merchants traded profitably. Within the empire, too, there were poor or sparsely inhabited areas that were simply passed by because they lacked tributary or strategic importance. Like a root system, the Aztec empire extended outward to the extent that it could draw nutrients from fertile soils; where this root system encountered rocks or infertile places, it simply grew around them.

The Aztec empire, however, was not fundamentally an empire of territory. It did not own lands with fixed borders that were circumscribed by hard edges. Instead, it was an empire of personal relationships. It took shape as a network of alliances, fealty, and tribute obligations between rulers, most of whom eventually came to be related to each other through marriage. Rulers who chose to join the empire before they were conquered were allowed to remain in power. Although they now worshipped Huitzilopochtli, hosted imperial officials, and sent tribute regularly (or provided military services), they kept a degree of autonomy; they still maintained their gods and their political power. Those sovereigns who resisted might be sacrificed to Huitzilopochtli and replaced as ruler by a member of the emperor's family, but the social and political structure of their polity would endure, and the alliance would be tied.

Set on a mountainside overlooking a valley southwest of Mexico-Tenochtitlan, the Temple of the Eagle and Jaguar Knights at Malinalco was one
The reconstructed conical thatched roof shades the entrance to the temple proper, a circular chamber carved into the living rock. The remains

4

THE EMPIRE'S PEOPLE

The net that held the Aztec empire together was its noble class, individuals of high birth who governed, administered, and reaped the greatest rewards from imperial expansion. Their livelihoods—and ultimately the empire's wealth—in turn relied on a vast and steady working class of commoners, most of whom farmed, fished, and toiled manually. Specialist skills came largely from a rising meritocracy of common-born craftspeople, merchants, and warriors. Additional labor came from a flexible system of

of the empire's important ceremonial centers.
of a sculpted jaguar guards the staircase.

Nobles, called *pipiltin*, considered themselves descendants of the first Mexica monarch. Nobles and commoners adhered to a strict dress code; no one could dress above his or her station. Noble clothing, as worn here by the Texcocan ruler Nezahualpilli, included elaborately decorated cloaks, loincloths of fine weave and design, and feathered hair ornaments. Jewelry was of gold, silver, and precious stones.

slavery. Each of these groups had many levels of social standing within it, but there was only one distinction that counted in Aztec society. A person was either a member of the nobility or a commoner, and the divide separated those who received from those who largely gave.

The nobles were the *pipiltin* (*pilli* in the singular), literally "children of someone [important]." Theirs was a hereditary status. As legitimate children of nobles on both sides, they considered themselves descendants of the first Mexica monarch, Acamapichtli. Thus, they traced their lineage through the Culhua back to the fabled Toltec lords of Tula. The Aztec princes told Father Sahagún that a noble person "has a mother, a father,...[is] virtuous, noble of birth, noble in way of life, humble, serious, modest, energetic, esteemed...good of heart, just, chaste, wise, prudent."

The pipiltin exercised considerable rights and privileges. They owned private, family lands that were worked by commoners, and they were supported by the commoners with both goods and services. As a matter of course, all the nobles would receive daily household provisions—such as corn, chilies, tomatoes, turkeys, wood—as well as the labor of men and women to haul water, make repairs, cook, and clean. Additional lands and additional benefits would come with higher social and administrative positions. The nobility wore exalted dress: cloaks of fine cotton, sandals, jewelry of precious materials and elaborate manufacture. Sumptuary laws set down by Moctezuma the Elder regulated a dress code for noble and commoner alike, so that one easily recognized each person's standing in the community. It was impossible to dress above one's position. These sumptuary laws, as written down in Durán's chronicle, even specified the kinds of fabrics and designs that could be used, and the length of a man's cloak.

Their children attended the *calmecac*, the school for noble children that was attached to the temples: girls to their own school and boys to theirs. Under strict priestly guidance, the children learned to live prudently, to understand the history and ways of their elders, to govern. In formal orations, the parents admonished their children: "Be not lazy, be not slothful.... Thou [goest] to be humble, to live austerely.... And do not gorge thyself with what thou eatest; be moderate. And do not clothe thyself excessively.... And take care [to understand] the writings, the books, the paintings. Enter with the prudent, the wise." Learning in the calmecac was essential for advancement within the imperial administration, whether it be in the priesthood or in the secular arm.

The perquisites of the nobility did not come alone. They were accompanied by obligations—both to the imperial government and to the commoners in their charge. Noblemen filled the ranks of clerks and officials, keeping tally of newly conquered lands, of warehouse stock, and of tribute owed. They were ministers, judges, and historians. Many served in the far reaches of the empire as hated tax collectors. Some rose in the military to join the prestigious Eagle

Knights and Jaguar Knights, the two military orders reserved only for nobles. Others traveled as envoys and ambassadors. Those who gained high rank were called *Tecuhtli* or Lord and were greatly esteemed. Noblewomen, whether married or not, wove the fine textiles required by the palaces and temples; some additionally became important but informal advisors to their husbands and sons who held office.

By virtue of their birth and achievement, some noblemen were chosen above others in their circle to rule. They were the *tlatoque*, or speakers, who, as proved statesmen and warriors, ruled the major towns and cities that their families had always controlled. The greatest of the tlatoque, the *Huey Tlatoani*, or Great Speaker, was the lord of Tenochtitlan, the emperor of the Aztec world who commanded the other tlatoque to his bidding. According to the formal rhetoric and the traditional orations, rule was less a privilege than it was a duty and a burden borne by the incumbent. Speeches made at the time a ruler took office tell how the previous rulers have "departed leaving the bundle, the carrying frame, the governed—heavy, intolerable, insupportable." The new ruler "will carry the load, he will bear the burden, he will reign. He will direct, he will guide. The commoner will respect him; [the ruler] will be his mother, his father. He will stop the tears of his vassals. He will bathe them, he will wash them. And he will determine their destruction, their exaltation."

While the ruler metaphorically carried the people on his back, the commoners were steadfast workers who provided the basic elements of food and shelter. Called *macehualtin* (*macehualli* in the singular), literally "workers," these tradespeople, peasants, and builders were the foundation of Aztec society and economy. In formal orations they are celebrated as "the common people, the humble eagle warriors, the humble jaguar warriors," or simply "the wing, the tail," who contributed no less than the seasoned warriors to Aztec success.

The rights of the macehualtin were few but significant. They were free people who had life interest in a plot of land, which could be passed down to their children. They participated with others in the ritual and civic life of their community, and they received their share when authorities distributed food and other goods. If they were intelligent and brave, they could rise in society and become relatively wealthy. Their children went to a local school, the *telpochcalli* (house of youth), where they were taught basic occupational skills, the elements of warfare, and good citizenship. By this, the children came to know the fundamentals of their history and religion, and to learn the valued characteristics of moderation, reverence, and valor. Bright children with promise might even be sent to the elite calmecac, where more emphasis was placed on scholarship in preparation for advanced careers.

Macehualtin were tied to their local communities and their lords by cords of service and taxation. They worked the lands of the nobility as well as

Long-distance merchants, or *pochteca*, such as the one pictured here, were a hereditary group within Aztec society that lived in special neighborhoods. The pochteca traded luxury items such as gold, jaguar skins, quetzal feathers, and other status symbols reserved for the elite. This detail, from a merchants' almanac in the *Codex Féjérváry-Mayer*, indicates that the day sign Dog, painted in front of the merchant, was auspicious for trade.

PREVIOUS PAGE: At one of the special schools called *calmecac*, the children of nobles and promising children of commoners studied arts and sciences, rhetoric, history, and divination, as well as the tenets of good citizenship. They also tended the temple with which the calmecac was affiliated, performed penances, and learned the appropriate ceremonies.

their own and served in labor drafts to build and maintain the nobles' palaces. Under their ruler's banner, they readily went to war. The taxes they paid supported community activities and services, much of it going also into tribute. Life was not easy for the peasant farmers in the hard-won provinces of the empire, for they bore the heaviest tribute burden. In contrast, the macehualtin of Tenochtitlan and the great allied cities of the lakeside must have felt themselves fortunate. Long ago many of them had left their fields for the trades and semi-skilled occupations that the metropolis required. As tribute poured in from the provinces, their tax burdens lessened, and they came to receive more than they paid.

Many macehualtin rose considerably above their brethren in status and wealth. Industrious and intelligent, or skilled and lucky, they commanded specialist skills or knowledge desired by the pipiltin and macehualtin alike. Brave and tough commoners who gained glory on the battlefield by taking prisoners could pursue the esteemed life of a successful warrior, rising in the military hierarchy to positions of prestige and power. Those knowledgeable of profits and the marketplace could rise from being local sellers to become rich merchants, or *pochteca*, the most revered being the long-distance pochteca who traded in high-cost, low-weight luxury goods far beyond the reaches of the empire. Intelligent youths fortunate enough to attend the calmecac could join the priesthood and fill some of the lower religious positions.

Slaves occupied the lowest level of the social scale. They worked without pay for masters who owned their work but not their persons, and who fed and clothed them. The children of slaves were born free. Slaves could buy their freedom or, having done so, could re-enter slavery during times of extreme poverty or famine. During the famine of the year 1 Rabbit, whole families sold themselves into slavery, as pictured here by Father Sahagún's artist. Both adults and children bear the wooden collars of their bondage.

15.

A macehualli with keen eyes, dexterous hands, and a fine aesthetic sense could become a valued artisan or *tolteccatl*. The name means craftsman, recalling the skill and artistry of the fabled Toltecs, who excelled in everything they attempted. Transforming precious raw materials into jewelry, ornaments, costumes, and artworks, the toltecca created the luxury goods that distinguished the pipiltin and symbolized imperial success. In a painted Texcocan history, the ruler Nezahualcoyotl is pictured together with all the different artisans who flocked to his city after he came to rule, transforming Texcoco into a brilliant artistic center. They include the painter, the grinder of pigments, the turquoise mosaic worker, the goldworker, the feather mosaic worker, the stone sculptor, and the woodcarver. The young pipiltin who worked with Father Sahagún described the tolteccatl as "well instructed, an artisan. There were many of them. ...[He] is accomplished, ingenious...imaginative, diligent...a possessor of knowledge...a designer of works of skill." The imperial cities drew skilled artisans to them like magnets.

These warriors, merchants, priests, and artisans composed a growing meritocracy of successful macehualtin. Many became wealthy, owning lands that were worked for them by tenant farmers and having slaves for labor. A few achieved high military and administrative positions and were accorded some of

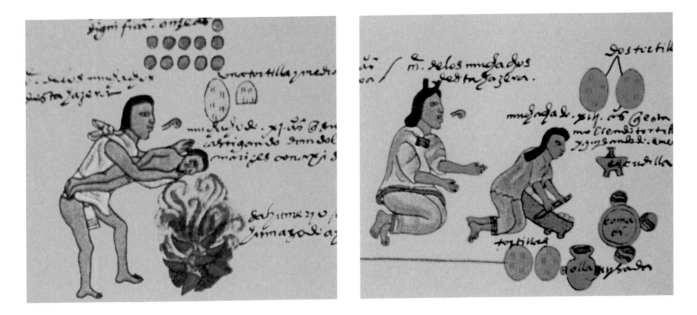

Fathers and mothers raised their children with care, making sure the children knew their responsibilities and mastered the necessary life skills. The extracts from the *Codex Mendoza* shown above and on the opposite page illustrate different experiences in the preparation for adulthood. From top left: a father holds his 11-year-old son over a fire of burning chilies as a punishment; a mother instructs her 13-year-old daughter how to grind corn and prepare the family meal; a young man exhibits skill at fishing; and a young woman weaves on a backstrap loom.

the privileges of the nobility, but even accomplished macehualtin remained distinct from the nobility by birth.

At the very bottom of the social and occupational scale came the slaves. An Aztec metaphor describes a slave as "malleable metal, a tumpline [a carrying rope], earth, mud, stone, wood, feathers, vine-weavings." These individuals were obliged to work without pay for others, who were required to feed and clothe them. In several respects, however, the Aztec institution of slavery differed from those elsewhere. An Aztec slave-owner owned the work of a slave, but not the person; the children of slaves were born free. Slaves could marry as they wished and could own land and property, including other slaves to work for them. Some slaves who worked as overseers of large estates even acquired considerable wealth themselves.

The institution was flexible; persons could enter and exit it. Individuals became slaves for specific periods of time to repay debts they incurred; gamblers and ne'er-do-well sons could easily lose themselves to slavery in this way. If a husband died when in debt, his wife or son might be forced into slavery to repay what he owed. Thieves were made to serve those whose goods they stole, until the worth of the goods had been repaid. Other crimes bound the culprits into slavery to the state. One could emerge from slavery by fulfilling one's obligation, or by buying oneself out of slavery. Families who owed slave labor to someone might replace one son with another until the obligation was fulfilled.

In times of extreme poverty or great hardship, people turned to slavery as a last resort for survival. During the disastrous famine of 1 Rabbit, many beleaguered families in the Valley of Mexico sold their children into slavery

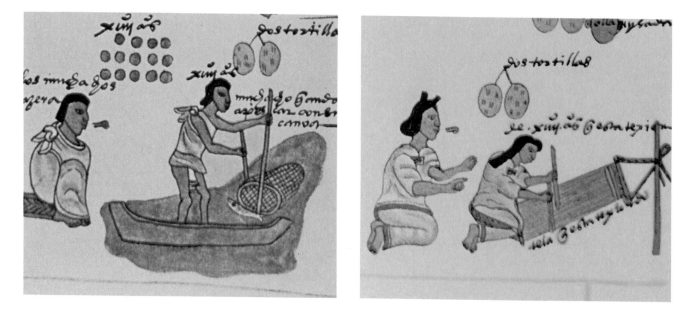

so that they would not starve. Later, when rains and prosperity came again, they hoped to buy their children back.

BONDS OF COMMUNITY

An Aztec was never alone. She or he always belonged to a household, a ward, and a community kingdom (town or city), and in these the individual found comfort and structure. The towns, as centers of the community, were clean and orderly places metaphorically and actually. They were places of social hierarchy and well-arranged architecture. They were places where one belonged to and with others, places of balance. Conversely, the edges and the terrain outside the community were thought of as being unbalanced and dangerous. Individuals who misbehaved were in danger of being exiled from their communities. An old adage recorded by Father Sahagún admonished: "If thou dost something [evil], thou wilt be driven forth, thou wilt be made to wander in others' enclosures, in the entrances of others' houses.... Thou wilt not wander to the city of another, nor canst thou longer dwell in thy city." An Aztec without a home and community "wandered as a rabbit, roamed as a deer," and perished.

The household was the primary locus of activity and culture. The basic unit was a husband, wife, and their dependents, for singles remained attached to their parents' households until they married and established their own households. There the division of labor was fairly evenly divided, the women being dedicated to the house and the men first to the battlefield and then to the fields or trade. Emblems given to newborn children symbolized these expectations: spinning and weaving equipment for the girls, and for the boys,

The Lienzo of Tequixtepec is a map of the community kingdom of that name, which is located in northern Oaxaca, far from the imperial heartland. Although the area was brought under Aztec control in the 1400s, it retained its Mixtec language and traditional pictorials. The upper two-thirds of the lienzo is a map of the territory, framed on the top and two sides by the boundary signs of the town. In the center, the founding couples are shown seated on jaguar thrones on top of the large, green place glyph of the town (Shell Hill). In registers below appear ancestral couples and scenes from the town's origin story. In the 1970s, local authorities allowed historian Ross Parmenter to photograph the lienzo, which they guard in the town archive.

four little arrows and a shield, plus the implements of a trade or livelihood. While the boys' umbilical cords were taken and buried on a battlefield, the girls' cords were buried next to the hearth, the focus of their activity.

Parents reared their children with great care and discipline. The *Codex Mendoza*, a manuscript painted shortly after the Conquest to explain Aztec ways, shows how the children were trained and how they developed from childhood to adulthood and old age. It also describes strict punishments meted out to wayward children. For vice and idleness, for instance, 11-year-olds could be held over burning chilies and made to breathe the sharp smoke. In training the young minds and guiding their development, parents were aided by the elders—the castigators and counselors—who, in elaborate and formal speeches called *huehuetlatolli* (literally "old-old speeches," or speeches of the elders), set out correct behavior. Many of these huehuetlatolli have come down to us, recorded by Spanish priests who were interested in the moral messages they imparted. The huehuetlatolli related ancient lore and admonished the young people to follow the ways of the ancients, to be

68

hardworking, prudent, and modest. They conveyed the importance of living and working as a member of a community: the good grandchild "provides fame and glory" to those around him; the bad grandchild "lives completely for himself, governs his own conduct, intercedes for himself, judges himself, needs no one."

For the larger events of their lives, the Aztecs interacted with the other families who lived in their neighborhoods, or *capulli* (literally "big houses;" singular is also capulli). These were the structured wards, barrios, or territories within which people generally both lived and worked. In most capulli, one could find members of all different occupations, noble and commoner alike, although some craft specialists such as featherworkers or goldworkers had their own capulli, as did the professional merchants of Tlatelolco.

Capulli life centered around the temple dedicated to its patron deity and the telpochcalli that trained its youths. The ceremonies and worship of the capulli god brought its members together. At the telpochcalli, the outstanding warriors of the barrio would lead instruction emphasizing the martial arts, sprinkled with lessons in history and religion. The capulli elders would give advice and counsel.

A major function of the capulli was to hold and portion out land. Its chief was an elected "elder," although not necessarily a noble. It was his duty to distribute lands according to need and availability and to keep the appropriate records. As the judge Alonso de Zorita carefully explained shortly after the Conquest, the capulli head "has pictures on which are shown all the parcels, and the boundaries, and where and with whose fields the lots meet, and who cultivates what field, and what [kind of] land each one has. The paintings also show which lands are vacant, and which have been given [out], and by and to whom and when they were given. The [elders] continually alter these pictures according to the changes worked by time." The capulli members met regularly in the elder's house to discuss "the group's needs and the payment of tribute, and to plan their festivals." This was always an expensive business, for the elder had to provide them with food and drink.

Aztecs belonged to households and capulli, but they took their fundamental identity from their town or polity. People belonged to an *altepetl* (the plural is *altepeme*). The word literally means "water-hill," a metaphoric reference to the water-filled mountain or mountain of sustenance, which gives life to the people. Although this reference is to territory, altepetl does not mean land so much as it means people. The altepetl carried with it a sense of ethnic distinctness. The Aztecs may have spoken the same language and shared a culture and way of life, but they did not consider themselves part of a larger ethnicity and culture. They thought of themselves not as Aztecs or Tepanecs, but as Mexica, as Texcoca, as Azcapotzalca, according to their altepetl.

This separate identity was as old as the people themselves. Each alteptl had its ancient histories that told of its people's emergence from a cave or descent from the Toltecs and then the long migration to their present home. Each also had its lineage books and its annals that kept track of events up to the present. Each people's story was different. Other people might be included if they affected the altepetl's history, but the focus stayed on the altepetl. The migration stories of the Mexica picture the other migrating groups, being careful to articulate and name each one, but they make it clear that they, the Mexica, followed their own route and underwent their own hardships. Small-town histories could be just as elaborate as those of the big cities. The poor and insignificant altepetl of Tepechpan in the northeast Valley of Mexico recorded its founding as grander than Tenochtitlan's, and earlier, too; its history painter, in an outpouring of altepetl pride, was even so bold as to run Tepechpan's history alongside and parallel to the history of the imperial capital, nicely equating the two.

An altepetl was a community kingdom, similar in many ways to a Mediterranean city-state like ancient Athens or Sparta. Geographically, it was composed of an urban core and the surrounding territory that supported it. A patron god guided the people, uniting them in worship. This deity stood metaphorically for the polity. When the imperial rulers Axayacatl and Tizoc had monuments carved to commemorate their victories over other altepeme, they presented themselves as Huitzilopochtli defeating the gods of the conquered towns. The hunting god Camaxtli lost the fight on behalf of Chalco, and the goddess Cihuacoatl embodied captured Xochimilco. Wars between altepeme became battles between altepetl gods.

Almost as important for an altepetl was its dynastic ruler, its tlatoani. Each altepetl had a noble family whose members had ruled the polity continuously since its migration or founding. These tlatoque were those "of the reed mat, the jaguar throne," who governed with full authority over their people; no other ruler would dare meddle in the internal affairs of an altepetl or attempt to circumvent the position of its tlatoani, unless he intended war. In theory, all tlatoani seats were equal, although the rulers of Tenochtitlan surely considered themselves superior to the tlatoque of polities like Tepechpan. It was the ruler's duty to lead the people in battle and at home, to keep the altepetl records, and to represent the altepetl in dealings with outsiders. He gathered tribute from the capulli heads for the altepetl and the empire, and he distributed any largess that arrived. He oversaw the temple and market place. He was the final authority in legal matters that came up from the courts. He was advised by a council of elders, who would choose his successor after he died.

These altepeme were the building blocks of the empire. Tribute came and went from them. In negotiations, on the battlefield, and in the tribute rolls, each altepetl remained a distinct entity. Each of its members found his

This gold lip-plug, styled in the form of a serpent, is typical of the gifts that an Aztec ruler bestowed on his vassals, warriors, and noblemen at great ceremonies and feasts. The Aztecs admired and copied the Mixtec tradition of goldworking; many Mixtec craftsmen came to work in Tenochtitlan.

and her identity there. The Triple Alliance succeeded in binding them together by various means, but they maintained their separateness.

NETWORK OF RULERS

The connecting fibers of the Aztec empire are found in the common interests of the altepetl rulers. Different polities may have been forced into the empire by threat of war or by conquest, but, once in, their rulers all became tied into a valuable network of tlatoque like themselves; enmity often dropped away. Membership brought the tlatoque strength and fellowship. Certainly the rulers were required to pay tribute, but they could simply increase the tribute they received from the mace-hualtin and pass on the surplus to the empire. Imperial policy was to maintain the local ruler and tribute system. If their neighbors gave them trouble, they could call on the imperial forces for assistance, as Tenantzingo did when it was squabbling with nearby Toluca.

The Aztec empire had virtually no infrastructure in its provinces. Imperial tax collectors would periodically appear in different areas to assure forthcoming tribute—as did those Cortés encountered in Veracruz—and, very occasionally, the emperor would replace a defeated local ruler with an imperial family member, but otherwise the bureaucracy was thin. The empire itself built no administrative centers, no imperial road system, and no network of royal storehouses, as other empires did elsewhere in the world. Instead, the rulers of Tenochtitlan and the other allied cities relied on the allegiance and self-interest of the local rulers to maintain the system. They bound the empire together by bringing the rulers into a network of familial relationships, economic benefits, and shared ideology.

The chronicles tell how, soon after a conquest, a royal marriage was almost always arranged, perhaps between one of the emperor's daughters and the ruler of the newly conquered territory. Polygamy was a perquisite of nobility, and the tlatoque in particular took many wives, thus tying themselves to other royal families. The Mexica rulers married wisely and often when they were still vassals to Azcapotzalco, linking themselves to powerful families in central Mexico. As they grew stronger, they continued the practice, making it increasingly difficult for other polities to revolt against their Mexica fathers, aunts, and cousins. Like royalty the world over, there came to be a great family of rulers.

Trade networks and warfare benefited the altepeme economically. Towns within the empire added lucrative long-distance trade ventures to their local markets and old trading patterns. This brought added income and luxury goods into the tlatoani palaces. Luxuries flowed to the provincial palaces after successful military campaigns, when spoils were distributed to the rulers and warriors of participating altepeme.

For the most part, the rulers throughout the empire were joined by a shared ideology and the strong sense of belonging to and participating in an elite group. This sense of participation was particularly manifest in great ceremonies that accompanied such state occasions as royal funerals, coronations, and the dedication of temples. Rulers from across the empire flocked to the elaborate celebrations hosted by the huey tlatoque of Tenochtitlan, whose feasts outshone all others. We have already noted how rulers from allied and enemy lands attended the sumptuous banquet and sacrifice that dedicated the Templo Mayor under Ahuitzotl. Even to inaugurate a single new sacrificial stone, however, the feasting and gift-giving were grand. Father Durán's chronicle records how Moctezuma the Elder "invited monarchs from the entire land.... Once the guests had arrived the king gave them presents—fine mantles and loin cloths, rich clothes of feather work, wide sashes, sandals and lip-plugs of precious stones, golden ear-plugs and nose pendants. A great feast followed, with quantities of fowl, meat from the hunt, different breads, chocolate drinks, and *pulque* [the native beer]." After the sacrifice, Moctezuma then distributed gifts of clothing, rich ornaments, and weapons to his warriors and noblemen.

No provincial could hope to match the display of Tenochtitlan, but ceremonies in other cities still attracted their distant peers. A provincial history notes that Ahuitzotl sent 40 sacrificial victims to help dedicate a new temple in Cuernavaca. Father Durán mentions that Moctezuma the Younger secretly attended or sent representatives to celebrations held by his bitter enemies the Tlaxcalans across the snowcapped volcanoes. A sense of noble obligation pervades these acts.

The majestic state ceremonies functioned in many ways as rituals of consumption and exchange. Rulers from close and distant towns would bring costly gifts to their host, as well as sacrificial victims for the ceremony. The imperial host then provided luxurious accommodations, abundant food, an elaborate ritual or sacrifice, and, finally, expensive gifts to departing guests.

Provincial tlatoque even in the farther reaches of the empire tried to emulate the imperial capital. Aztec modes of dress spread to distant tlatoani seats, along with styles of stone carving and finely painted ceramics. Father Durán's history describes how, after the dedication of a Sun Stone with

The circular temple at Malinalco is one of the most impressive Aztec monuments to have survived the Spanish Conquest. Carved into the circular bench are a jaguar pelt and two eagle skins. In the center of the floor is a third carved eagle. Here in this man-made cave, warriors and lords would gather for rituals that endorsed imperial authority.

attendant sacrifices to the sun, "the dignitaries of the neighboring cities then returned to their homelands eager to imitate the Mexica. They began to build pyramids and sacrifice men in a similar way, to elect and form a priesthood to practice these rites." At Malinalco in Morelos, provincial stonecutters carved into the hillside a circular temple dedicated to the Eagle Knights and Jaguar Knights. They worked in the imperial sculptural style to bring metropolitan ideology and aesthetics to the countryside. Powerfully carved wooden drums from the same area look like they could easily have come from Tenochtitlan's workshops. In Veracruz in the east, and in Tlapa in southern Guerrero, provincial manuscript painters adopted the painting traditions of the Aztec heartland; they told their own stories, and they painted in the Aztec style. The Aztec empire did not so much force its customs and styles on others as the provincials consciously adopted the ways of the capital. Nobles in the provinces wanted to keep their internal autonomy, but they also wanted to demonstrate that they, too, belonged to the Aztec network.

Some of the chinampa plots constructed by the Aztecs on marshland outside Tenochtitlan are still in use today. The chinampas were built up

etation, their edges anchored by pylons and willow trees, and yielded several crops a year. Canals, like the one used by this Mexican farmer,

with layers of fertile lake mud and decaying veg-
facilitated the transport of crops to Tenochtitlan.

5

LIVING WELL AND PROSPERING

When Moctezuma the Younger sat down to dinner, it was to a bountiful feast. Samples of all the foods in the land were before him. Bernal Díaz remembers there being more than 300 different dishes: the meats of so many kinds of birds and beasts that the conqueror could not name them all, plus fish, vegetables, and fruit of all descriptions. There were tortillas and maize cakes. All were served on delicate ceramic dishes made across the mountains in Cholula, and set on a low table covered with fine cloths. Moctezuma's servants then brought him frothy chocolate drinks in cups of pure gold followed by tubes of tobacco for the ruler's smoke. Jesters, singers, and dancers entertained him. The huey tlatoani of the Aztec empire was prosperous indeed.

Such a dinner was not a banquet for hundreds of pipiltin, or nobles, attending a state occasion, but an ordinary affair of the kind often repeated in the royal palace. Still, it drew on the empire's entire economic system. Produce and grains came from agricultural fields dispersed over different ecozones. Fish and other water animals came from the valley lakes, from distant rivers, and even from the eastern sea. Swift relay runners brought fresh fish from the Gulf of Mexico to Moctezuma's table. Farms and forests provided the savory meats of domesticated animals and game. From cotton fields, woodlands, and distant mines came the raw materials for the fabrics, table, and tableware. A complex collection system of trade and tribute then delivered these raw materials into the hands of skilled artisans who fashioned the vessels and dishes that so impressed the conquerors. The wealth and economic organization of the empire brought all these together for Moctezuma's dinner, and, as Bernal Díaz remarked, "his expenses must have been considerable."

For the macehualtin who grew the produce, worked in the mines, and crafted the cups and plates, dinners were incomparably simpler. There was none of the finery and only a few dishes. Even a modest Aztec dinner, however, relied on the products and labor of others; no family was fully self-sufficient. There was always a reason to go to the marketplace, either to acquire foods one could not grow or to barter for such goods as cutting implements, grinding stones, or pottery.

ALL THE FOOD NECESSARY FOR THEM

When Father Sahagún set out to list "all [the] food necessary" for the Aztecs, and how it was arranged for sale in the marketplace, he naturally began with "maize, white, black, red, and yellow." Maize or corn was far and away the mainstay of the Aztec diet, followed by beans—"yellow beans, white ones, black, red, pinto beans, large beans"—and grains such as amaranth and chia. Other dietary staples came from the lake, vegetable garden, and "barn yard." From the arid slopes and plains, cacti had seemingly endless uses.

A banquet scene from the *Florentine Codex* depicts women of the nobility enjoying a variety of dishes. Pictured are meat dishes or stews served in wide, three-footed bowls, as well as steamed tamales served in baskets. The Aztec diet was largely vegetarian, supplemented by animal protein from game, fish, turkeys, dogs, and invertebrates such as worms or insects. The empire's well-developed trading economy, together with the Aztec system of tribute, helped to ensure well-stocked markets.

Corn had been grown in the Valley of Mexico for more than 5000 years, and had long been the inhabitants' principal food. Like the Toltecs before them, the Aztecs put corn tortillas at the center of their diet. Parents judged the nutritional needs of their growing children in terms of the number of tortillas they ate. However, wives and mothers also prepared corn tamales in a great variety of ways, and made a corn gruel called *atolli*, seasoned with many different ingredients. The corn harvest was so important that a whole cluster of deities watched over it. The storm god Tlaloc and the goddess of ground water, Chalchiuhtlicue (Jades Her Skirt), watered the fields; Xilonen (Young Maize Ear) looked over the tender green ears of the young plants, Centeotl (Maize Cob Lord) and Chicomecoatl (Seven Serpent) protected the ripening ears. The Aztecs thought of Chicomecoatl, the principal corn goddess, as "our sustenance...our flesh, our livelihood;...[she] maketh all our food." In another metaphor, they spoke of an ear of corn as "an ear of [precious] metal, a jade, a bracelet—precious, our flesh, our bones."

In the diet, chia and amaranth shared many of the properties of corn and filled the critical gap between corn harvests. Aztec cooks made a nourishing chia gruel and a good amaranth tamale. From the ground seeds of one variety of amaranth, the priests formed dough images of the gods. Even today in Mexico, amaranth seed cakes, flavored with honey and often modeled as figures, are sold at festivals and along pilgrimage routes; they are called *alegría*, or joy. Beans of many kinds, squash, tomatoes, other vegetables, and the ever-present chilies rounded out the harvests. The *nopal*, or prickly pear cactus, yielded both juicy fruits (*tunas*) and tender palms that could be eaten cooked or raw.

From the lake, hunters took ducks, geese, and other birds. Watermen and fisherwomen caught fish, frogs, salamanders, shrimp, and waterflies. Meaty lizards were "good, fine; edible; savory; what one deserves." The green scum of waterfly eggs that formed on the lake was gathered to make "a kind of bread" that Bernal Díaz said "tastes rather like cheese."

More dietary protein came from domesticated turkeys, which supplied the most meat, and domesticated dogs. Hunters brought in deer, peccaries, rabbits, hares, pheasants, and other game. Gatherers collected lizards, grasshoppers, grubs, and worms; Aztec palates particularly enjoyed certain insects as "savory, good to the taste."

There has been much scholarly argument about human flesh as an Aztec food, and the idea is basically false. The notion that human flesh was an important protein resource for the Aztecs has been bandied about, generally by those who don't understand the place of cannibalism in Aztec life. The conquerors do not help; before they arrived in Mexico, they had all heard about cannibalism in the Antilles, and they readily assumed the Aztecs thought and acted the same way. They roundly accused the Aztecs of cannibalism, mostly to justify their ill-treatment of them, but they offered very little evidence. Cortés defended his enslavement of the Aztecs by saying that "they are all cannibals, of which I send Your Majesty no evidence because it is so infamous." Bernal Díaz repeats a rumor he had heard that Moctezuma used to eat "the flesh of young boys," but he admits he couldn't himself tell one meat dish from another.

Cannibalism on a very limited level had a place in a handful of religious celebrations. During the rites for one of the monthly feasts, war captives were presented by their captors for sacrifice. Then the bodies were carried back to their captors' neighborhood, and cooked, and the meat subsequently was distributed to residents in a special feast. He who had taken the captive, however, could not partake, because the slain captive, metaphorically, was his "beloved son," his "very self." Motolinía points out that human flesh was eaten mostly by the lords, priests, and merchants, but not often by the macehualtin. The lords, priests, and merchants were the principal actors in religious ceremonies; their consumption of human flesh occurred within the

Corn was the staple of Aztec life, the basic ingredient for tortillas, a variety of tamales, and a gruel called atolli. Illustrations from Father Sahagún's *Florentine Codex* depict farmers planting, tending, and harvesting corn. The Aztecs honored this crop at every stage of growth, invoking several deities to protect the harvest.

ritual context. In all the 16th-century descriptions of Aztec ritual, cannibalism is mentioned for only a few ceremonies.

The Aztecs took their animal protein mainly from domesticated turkeys and dogs, as well as from rabbits and birds they shot, and from those small, tasty creatures they gathered. An even greater proportion of their protein came from the combination of maize and beans in their diet.

If corn was the foundation for Aztec subsistence, the maguey cactus was the multipurpose tool. The Aztecs used maguey products for a great many purposes. Father Motolinía, who devoted an entire chapter of his history to the uses of the maguey plant, remarked that "as many things are made of it as are said to be made of iron." Maguey was farmed on arid hillsides and plains where there was not enough rainfall for other crops. Its sap made a refreshing drink. Fermented, the sap became *pulque*, the native beer and principal intoxicant, against which so many Aztecs were warned. Unfermented sap could be converted into maguey syrup, an important sweetener in a land without cane sugar, and into medicines. Fibers from the leaves became sewing thread, cords, and ropes. Maguey fiber was beaten into paper and woven into mantles, clothing, and footwear; the merchants traveled in cloaks of netted maguey fiber, and the macehualtin wore maguey-fiber clothes. Cooks used pieces of maguey leaves to catch corn when it was being ground; artisans prized sections of leaf as workboards and supports for their art. Dried leaves became firewood, and the thick stalks replaced wood in houses where timber was scarce. The spines were used as needles, punches, and tacks. In temple precincts and palaces across the land, priests and rulers would draw great maguey spines through their flesh in bloodletting ceremonies. From the poorest commoner to the high priest of Tenochtitlan, all relied on the versatile maguey plant. Maguey was the only crop other than corn to be represented by its own deity. The goddess Mayahuel, she of the

Maguey, a fleshy-leafed agave cactus, was cultivated in Aztec times, as it is today, for a wide variety of uses. Chief among these was *pulque*, a type of beer made from the plant's fermented sap. Maguey products also included rope, clothing, footwear, building materials, firewood, and even a sweetener. The sharp spines of the cactus were used by Aztec priests for ritual bloodletting. Maguey was so important to Aztec life that it had its own deity, a bountiful goddess named Mayahuel.

400 (or innumerable) breasts, personified the bountiful maguey; her children, the 400 Rabbits of pulque, were gods of drunkenness and medicine.

Although maguey needed little attention once it was planted, most other crops required fertile soil and regular supplies of water. Where rainfall was marginal, Aztec farmers built and maintained irrigation systems. In and around the lake they constructed chinampa plots, those miracles of agriculture that could yield several crops a year. In the sweetwater marshes and swamps, farmers created raised chinampa fields by piling up mud and vegetation between pylons and digging canals in between. Later, they planted willow trees on the margins of the fields because the willows' long roots would continue to contain the earth. On a regular basis, mud dredged from the bottom of the canals added nutrients to the soil and kept the waterways open. Although the chinampas did not float, as some have said, they are popularly called "floating gardens." Chinampas are still cultivated in Xochimilco (Flower Field), south of Mexico City, where they are a popular attraction for families at leisure.

In Aztec times, chinampas surrounded Tenochtitlan and the other cities in and around the sweetwater part of Lake Texcoco. They were concentrated especially in the south, where the rich agricultural communities of Xochimilco, Chalco, and Cuitlahuac formed the "bread basket" for

Tenochtitlan. These chinampa cities contributed between a quarter and a half of all the dietary needs of Tenochtitlan. Chinampa plots in Tenochtitlan itself were smaller and were cultivated principally for fresh vegetables and flowers.

BASIC GOODS AND LUXURY CRAFTS

Although chinampa farmers labored full-time on their plots, most other agriculturists supplemented their livelihood with a part-time specialization, either producing goods from raw materials or extracting the raw materials themselves. They had time between duties to their fields, and they could always use the extra income to offset a poor harvest or add new goods. The chroniclers do not speak about these rural specialists, but the archaeological record does.

In Huexotla, in the northeast Valley of Mexico, archaeologist Elizabeth Brumfiel found large numbers of tools and waste materials belonging to several Aztec manufacturing or extracting industries. The artifacts were not so concentrated that they represented full-time specialization. Instead, the scatter told of part-time cottage industries that produced goods needed by the ordinary citizen. The maguey-products industry was represented by stone blades of the kind used to separate out the maguey fibers, scrapers and jars used to get maguey syrup, and spindle whorls for spinning maguey and cotton thread. Arrow points told of deer hunting, and small, clay, blowgun pellets had been used to hunt rabbits and birds. There at Huexotla, farming families produced the kind of goods their neighbors could use, the kind they could trade in the local market.

Elsewhere the pattern is the same. In nearby Teotihuacan, the concentration of obsidian cores from the Aztec period examined by archaeologist Michael Spence tells of part-time specialists producing obsidian blades for exchange. Ceramics analyzed by archaeologist Mary Hodge in the southern valley were made locally and traded within the regional market. The average macehualtin could go to the market and expect that most of the goods there—the pottery, obsidian, grinding stones, salt, mineral

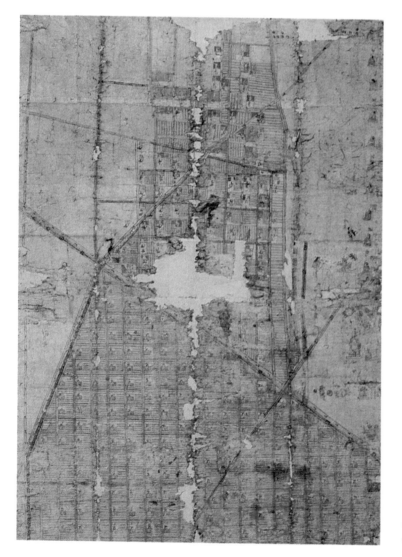

The chinampas were laid out as parallel rows of long, narrow plots. The 16th-century Maguey Plan—so-called because it is painted on maguey-fiber paper—shows a typical chinampa district of Tenochtitlan; each plot's occupant is indicated by a small house crowned with the head and name glyph of its farmer.

Aztec goldworkers learned much of their art from highly skilled Mixtec craftsmen from Oaxaca. The necklace shown here features tiny gold skulls with moveable jaws, separated by disks of turquoise. Very little Aztec gold has come down to us, because the Spaniards melted down as much as they could after the invasion. Archaeologists have not found rich, gold-laden Aztec tombs in the imperial heartland, because the Aztecs traditionally cremated their elite dead. The gold jewelry that has survived comes largely from Mixtec and Zapotec tombs in Oaxaca; it shows great delicacy and exquisite workmanship.

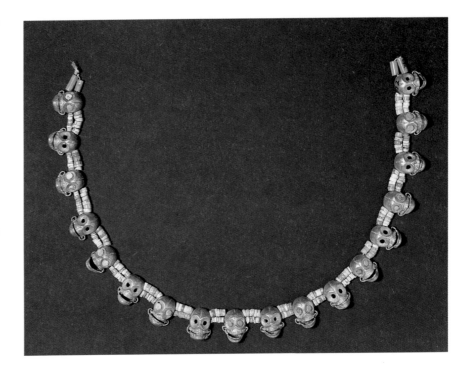

lime, and cotton, as well as foods and medicines of various kinds—were made or mined by part-time specialists like themselves.

Full-time specialization developed where the skills required by a job were great or where the raw materials were costly. Father Sahagún's noble informants thought of some specialties as being more similar than others; they grouped together the carpenters, stonecutters, masons, scribes, singers, wisemen (owners of books), physicians, soothsayers (those who read the day signs), and attorneys. All these specialties required much expertise, but the tools and materials being used were not necessarily expensive. In an entirely different category were the luxury artisans, the toltecca. They were gold workers, coppercasters, lapidaries, turquoise-mosaic workers, feather workers, specialist weavers, and producers of rabbit-fur garments and cloth. Most of these artisans were drawn to the cities, where they produced goods for the rulers and nobility. Their products were items of clothing, personal ornaments, and costumes for war and religious celebrations. They either worked directly in the rulers' households or worked independently on commission.

The Spanish chroniclers are universal in their praise of Aztec luxury products. Cortés, referring to the gold and silver jewelry, featherwork, and precious stones he took from Moctezuma the Younger, wrote to Charles V: "All these, in addition to their intrinsic worth, are so marvelous that considering their novelty and strangeness they are priceless; nor can it be believed that any of the princes of this world, of whom we know, possess any things of such high quality." Of the

Featherworking was a sophisticated craft among the Aztecs, who valued feathered articles more highly than those made of gold, silver, or jade. The long, green tail feathers of the quetzal were difficult to obtain even in Aztec times; nevertheless, feather workers used them in great quantities for such sumptuous headdresses as the one shown at right, which Cortés shipped home as a gift for Charles V. The bright blue feathers used here come from the blue cotinga.

The feathers on this small shield, or disk, were cut to create the design of a swirl of blue water with smaller eddies within it. In the center, grey feathers form a rectangular patch of cultivated earth, pierced by a yellow digging stick.

gold and silver he said that "no smith in the world could have done better;" he described the jewels as "so fine that it is impossible to imagine with what instruments they were cut so perfectly," and the feathers as "more wonderful than anything in wax or embroidery." Even Father Motolinía's vow of poverty did not keep him from admiring the inventiveness of Aztec gold and silverworkers, who, he said, "surpass the silversmiths of Spain" in their skill and ingenuity.

The Europeans prized the gold, silver, and jewels, but the Aztecs themselves valued the featherwork more highly. The brilliant feathers that composed cloaks and shields, headdresses, and fans came as tribute from the most distant provinces, or were acquired at great risk and cost by long-distance traders. The blue cotinga, whose luminescent blue feathers were used to make the costume of Huitzilopochtli, could not be captured barehanded, but had to be seized with a handful of green grass, for, as Sahagún's noble informants told him, "if only with the hands one were to take it, then the blue cotinga's feathers were blemished; the blue became as if soiled." Equally difficult to acquire were other birds, such as the quetzal from the mountain valleys of Guatemala, whose long twin tail feathers of iridescent green went into headdresses and standards. Feather workers who mastered the difficult process of gluing or

This double-headed serpent pectoral is made of hollowed wood covered with turquoise mosaic. The technique of turquoise mosaic was well developed among the Mixtecs of Oaxaca: finished mosaic pieces and turquoise chips featured prominently in the lists of tribute rendered by southern vassal states.

tying each feather into place within its design were artisans of the highest rank; the chroniclers describe them as being both men and women, the latter concentrating on feather cloaks and garments. The products they created met all the criteria by which Aztecs judged preciousness: they were artfully designed, brilliantly colored, costly, and fragile.

Featherwork, perhaps even more than the other luxury products, was indispensable for all state ritual occasions. At those times, the cult images, deity impersonators, rulers, nobles, and warriors would be costumed in feather garments. Featherwork was equally necessary for the proper conduct of war, because no great warrior could go into battle inappropriately costumed. Elite warrior costumes were covered with feathers. An Aztec proverb speaks of "the precious feathers of the lord," for featherwork was the purview of the nobility.

POCHTECA

These feathers arrived in the palaces and marketplaces on the backs of human porters who had trekked the paths and roads under the watchful eyes of long-distance merchants, or *pochteca*. For 15 miles (24 kilometers) a day, these porters could bear 50 pounds (22.6 kilograms) on their carrying frames, supported by tumplines from their foreheads. In a land without beasts of burden or wheeled vehicles, human porters were essential to any overland venture.

The long-distance pochteca who organized caravans were among the most highly respected of macehualtin. They were the agents who acquired much of the raw materials necessary for the luxurious clothing and ornaments of the nobility. They set out with finished luxury goods and local products—fine clothing and jewelry, obsidian, and rabbit fur—to trade for raw materials. They brought home the feathers of tropical birds, jade, turquoise, spondyllus and other shells, and the skins of exotic animals. The Aztec rulers valued their services and rewarded the pochteca accordingly. Moctezuma the Elder and his successors showered the principal merchants with gifts and allowed them to sacrifice slaves, to own land that was worked by others, and to wear symbols of noble status on ceremonial occasions. For their own part, the elite merchants did not abuse these special privileges. They lived humbly, abasing themselves in public; as Sahagún's informants recalled, "they did not seek honor and fame. They walked about wearing only their miserable maguey fiber capes." It was a good strategy for those who did not want to appear in competition with their noble clients. Their main outlets for displays of status were elaborate ceremonies the principal merchants hosted periodically at great expense.

Long-distance merchants were also called vanguard merchants, disguise merchants, and spying merchants. Upon entering enemy territory, the Aztec traders might take on the appearance of the locals, cutting their hair, wearing the costume, and even learning the native language. This allowed them greater freedom of movement and anonymity. In enemy lands they were watchful and observant, returning with news to retell before the Aztec emperor. Indeed, Aztec rulers occasionally sent the vanguard merchants forth as spies into regions of battle. As individuals who served the military interests of the empire, such vanguard merchants earned their status as eagles and jaguars, who, dying on the road, would become companions of the sun.

THE MARKETPLACE

Those goods that did not go directly to the palaces came to the markets. Regional markets—held regularly in various locations every 5, 13, or 20 days—satisfied most ordinary needs of the macehualtin. As is the case today, however, the largest selection and finest workmanship was found in the markets of the big cities. The chinampa cities of Xochimilco, Chalco, and Cuitlahuac hosted major markets; Texcoco's market was even larger. The greatest market in the Aztec realm, however, was in Tlatelolco. This was the market that so astounded Bernal Díaz and impressed Hernán Cortés when they saw it. There, all manner of goods were presented, each in its own section; officials patrolled the area to ensure that no one was being cheated, and market judges called for stiff sentences for thieves and frauds.

Cortés described the Tlatelolco marketplace as being "twice as big as that of Salamanca, with arcades all around, where more than sixty thousand people come...to buy and sell, and where every kind of merchandise produced in these

Long-distance trade brought luxury goods to a noble clientele, and bestowed high status on the long-distance merchants, or *pochteca*. This image from the *Florentine Codex* shows two such merchants displaying their wares. The top one is offering richly woven cloaks and huipils, gold lip-plugs and ear-spools, gold rings, and gold diadems. The merchant below him displays obsidian lip-plugs and blades, golden needles and bells, and a skein of dyed rabbit fur for weaving.

The great market at Tlatelolco, shown here in a reconstruction in Mexico's National Museum of Anthropology, was the commercial heart of the empire. Long-distance merchants brought luxury goods from every corner of the empire to be bartered here, and farmers offered fresh food and flowers grown on the surrounding chinampas. To keep the market orderly and honest, the Aztecs kept a tight rein on its activities. Judges were on hand to settle price disputes.

lands is found; provisions as well as ornaments of gold and silver, lead, brass, copper, tin, stones, shells, bones, and feathers. They also sell lime, hewn and unhewn stone, adobe bricks, tiles, and cut and uncut woods of various kinds. There is a street where they sell game and birds of every species found in this land: [turkeys], partridges and quails, wild ducks.... They sell rabbits and hares, and stags and small gelded dogs which they breed for eating."

Cortés spoke of streets of herbalists, barbers, and restaurants. There was "firewood and charcoal, earthenware braziers and [reed] mats;" there was cotton in every color, "like the silk market at Granada, except here there is a much greater quantity." Every sort of vegetable was offered, along with honey, syrup, and wax. Vendors sold ground corn, tortillas, fish, and eggs. They sold paints and animal skins. The goods offered in Tlatelolco were so many and so varied that Cortés could not remember them all. He remarked that "each kind of merchandise is sold in its own street without any mixture whatever.... Everything is sold by number and size.... There is...a very large building like a courthouse, where ten or twelve persons sit as judges. They preside over all that happens in the markets, and sentence criminals. There are in this square other persons who walk among the people to see what they are selling and the measures they are using."

The Aztecs poured into the Tlatelolco market for both goods and services. This was the place to acquire raw materials, but it was also the place to hire a carpenter, a singer, or a scribe. Cortés did not mention the prostitutes or those who did repair work, but these people also had their sections of the market. Marketplace exchange worked on a barter system, but monies in the form of cacao beans and large white cotton cloaks could facilitate the actual transaction. The cloaks had the higher value, equal to 100 or more cacao beans, depending on the cloak. Aztecs sometimes expressed wealth in terms of these cloaks: a man could live for a year on the value of 20 cloaks.

As is the case today, the markets of the Aztec empire attracted men, women, and entire families, who sought to acquire and exchange things and who enjoyed the community a marketplace offered. Markets were places to gather, to see one's neighbors, to learn the latest news, and to gossip. Aztecs attended the markets to which they had political and community ties, not necessarily those that were geographically closest to them, for the markets were an integral part of the community kingdoms. Although the markets were self-policed, they came under the jurisdiction of the local rulers, who extracted a tax on the goods and services exchanged.

IMPERIAL TRIBUTE

Although the market network bolstered the imperial economy, tribute was the economic factor that kept the empire solvent. The tribute system brought into the valley the subsistence goods needed to help feed the populations of Tenochtitlan, Texcoco, and Tlacopan. It also brought the luxury goods that were so critical to the nobility as markers of status. The limits of human porters meant that grains, wood, and other heavy commodities came from nearby provinces, while the high-cost, low-bulk luxury goods came from farther away.

Several Aztec tribute lists have survived from the 16th century, having been preserved in Mexican and European archives. After the Conquest, the Spanish Crown took a great interest in the tribute Moctezuma received; specifically, it wanted to know who paid what, and how often, in order to set its own demands accordingly. The Spanish king asked that all the tribute registers be sent to him or copied for him, and quite a number apparently were. Those that have survived help us understand how the empire was organized and give a detailed picture of what each province paid the imperial tax collectors.

The *Codex Mendoza* is such a document, copied by an Aztec painter from older documents and annotated with Spanish explanations. It was commissioned by Viceroy Mendoza for Charles V, but the ship that was to take it to Spain was captured by French pirates, and the codex eventually found its way to England.

Vassal states were required to send tribute to the imperial center. The tribute rendered to Tenochtitlan by the nearby province of Chalco is represented graphically on this page of the *Codex Mendoza*. A jade disc, the place sign for Chalco, appears at top left; below it are the place signs for the other towns in the province. To its right are symbols for bundles of white cloaks: the feather above each denotes 400 such cloaks. Also depicted are two warrior costumes, complete with shields, and along the bottom, containers representing food from the chinampas.

For each province delivering tribute, the artist painted the name glyphs or place signs of the relevant towns on the left side of the page, beginning with the provincial capital at the top. To the right, he drew the kind and quantity of tribute.

Chalco, pictorially represented by the jade disk which is its name, sent mostly grains, as befits a chinampa province. The semi-annual tribute begins at the top of the page with loads of large white cloaks; the stylized feathers above each cloak mean 400, so that Chalco paid 400 x 2, or 800, loads of these cloaks. It also sent two complete warrior costumes, with shields, all of fine

Luxury goods, such as quetzal feathers, jaguar skins, amber, and gold, came from the distant province of Xoconosco, represented here in the upper left corner by its place sign, a nopal cactus. Conquered in the late 15th century, Xoconosco was a collection point for these high-cost, low-bulk commodities from Guatemala. At the top of this particular tribute list are two necklaces of jade, followed by bundles of feathers, gold lip-plugs, jaguar skins, bags of cacao, and, at the bottom, two large blocks of amber.

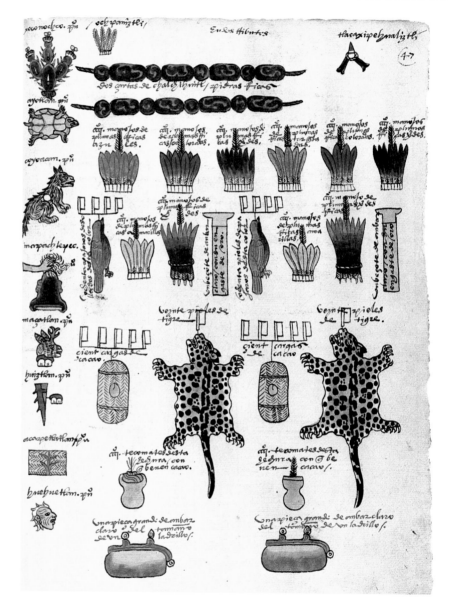

feathers, and—most importantly—great wooden bins of corn, beans, chia, and amaranth—solid food from the nearby chinampa fields.

Distant Xoconosco, the collection point for exotic materials of the Maya rain forest, sent luxury goods. Only recently had Moctezuma the Younger succeeded in bringing it into the empire and adding its goods to the flow. The artist painted two necklaces of jade beads, followed by 6 x 400 bundles of colored feathers (blue, red, and green). In the next row, the little flags or banners mean 20, making the tribute 4 x 20 x 2 (160) pelts of the blue cotinga, 400 x 2 (800) bundles of yellow feathers, 400 x 2 bundles of the long green tail feathers of the quetzal, and two lip-plugs of amber set in gold. There follow 200 loads of cacao beans, 40 jaguar skins, 800 gourd bowls in two shapes for drinking chocolate, and two large pieces of clear amber the size of a brick.

The tribute-paying provinces sent the products for which they were best known. Cotton and cacao came from the hot lowland regions, gold from the mines of Guerrero, and turquoise from the mountains of western Oaxaca. Additionally, almost every province was required to send a certain number of completed warrior costumes. This meant that every province had to acquire the feathers, the precious metals, and the fine stones that composed the costumes, and had to support the artisans who created them. This effectively spread the warrior costume industry throughout the empire. It stimulated the market economy by forcing provinces to trade for feathers and other luxury goods, and it created centers of artisanry in the provinces.

In all, an extraordinary amount of tribute flowed into the imperial capital. Much of it was redistributed to other rulers to cement alliances throughout the empire, and to those who attended the elaborate state ceremonies. It went also to the individual warriors for their service. Some tribute left the city on the backs of merchants' porters to be exchanged for distant exotic goods. The bulk, however, remained in the capital city, supporting all the many parts of the palaces and temples.

MOCTEZUMA'S PALACE

The royal palace at the time the Spaniards arrived was a complex and opulent place. Motolinía speaks of Moctezuma's innumerable attendants, "who were like blades of grass in the field." Bernal Díaz tells how more than 600 lords and nobles would come each day with their servants. In residence at any given time were members of the extensive royal family, plus ambassadors, judges, and high priests. The eldest sons of provincial rulers were in Moctezuma's service, as were many of the daughters, who wove fine cloths for the palace and temples. High-ranking warriors, scholars, and advisors counted as part of the household. Luxury artisans (men and women), workmen, and performers of all kinds worked and lived within the palace walls. The priests who managed the temples were fed from palace kitchens. Bernal Díaz recalled that after Moctezuma dined, more than a thousand plates were brought for his guards and household servants.

Moctezuma the Younger's palace was so grand that Hernán Cortés found it "impossible to describe its excellence and grandeur." He knew of nothing in Spain with which to compare it. Sixteenth-century paintings of this and other Aztec palaces indicate a large central courtyard entered on one side and surrounded on all four sides by large halls opening into the center. The building was of stonework, plastered and painted. Cotton or feather textiles hung in the broad post-and-lintel doorways to give privacy where desired; on the floors,

Moctezuma's palace adjoined the sacred precinct of Tenochtitlan and covered an estimated 6 acres (2.4 hectares). His private apartments were located above the royal council chambers. A page from the *Codex Mendoza* shows the ruler himself inside, while his advisers meet downstairs. As *tlatoani*, or ruler, Moctezuma had military, religious, and social duties: he was head of state, commander of the Aztec armies, and a vital link between the gods and his people.

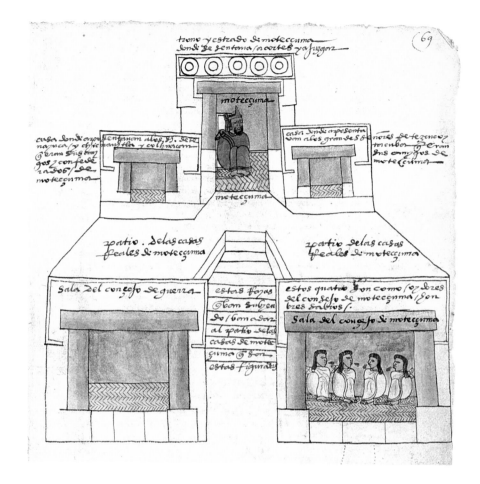

woven reed mats provided bedding and seating. Concentrated on the ground floor were the administrative rooms, including the great council halls where the high court convened and the war council met. There, too, were the quarters for servants and retainers, and the storage facilities. On a second floor, approached from the patio by an outside stairway, were the emperor's personal quarters, the family rooms, and extensive guest quarters for his allies and visitors. Moctezuma the Younger's palace, built because his father's palace was too small, covered an estimated 6 acres (2.4 hectares).

An accounting office kept record of all the tribute that arrived. The palace also boasted an armory, where the feathered warrior costumes shimmered brightly, and a treasury, which the Spaniards were delighted to discover. An aviary housed birds from all over the land; a house of carnivores, not quite a zoo, kept beasts of prey; a large pleasure garden contained flowers, herbs, baths, and streams for the ruler's enjoyment. The palace was an elaborate and costly organism maintained by the tribute from the provinces and the allegiance of their rulers.

The Calendar Stone, or Stone of the Sun, depicts the fifth and present age of humankind. The large rectangular panels surrounding the central
preceding ages, and form the X-shaped sign of the present age, 4 Movement. The 20 day signs, the rays of the sun, and two great fire serpents

face of the earth, or night sun, represent the four
ring this sign in concentric circles.

6

THE COSMIC ORDER

The Aztec world was alive with spirit and meaning. Rocks, ears of corn, the wind in the evening—all were animate to the extent that they possessed essences that could affect humankind, and all had self-will. All aspects of nature had been created by deities or supernatural forces that still resided there. Every part of the world was something to be reckoned with, and it was an Aztec's obligation to go through life in negotiation with these forces. The wind, for example, was embodied as Ehecatl, "the roadsweeper of the rain gods," who could intensify, roar, and grow wrathful. Ears of corn in the fields could shrivel to nothing unless they were addressed in song and cajoled to ripen well; rain alone would not ensure a bountiful harvest if the appropriate offerings were not made. Even with all the proper rituals, however, the world could be a difficult place.

An episode in Father Durán's history shows just how contrary the world could be. The emperor Moctezuma the Younger wished to embellish the ritual precinct of Tenochtitlan with a new gladiatorial stone on which warriors and war captives would do ritual battle. His representatives scoured the land to find a great rock suitable for such a monument and finally located one outside of Chalco. Stonecutters from six cities gathered there to scrape it clean and prepare to tear it from its bed. "Since it was a sacred thing," priests and singers made offerings to it; "going round and round they incensed it with much ceremony, pouring molten incense and liquid rubber upon it, killing quail and splashing the blood upon the rock." The great rock would not budge, however; it broke all the poles and stout ropes. Reinforcements were called in from Texcoco. With additional ritual offerings and much straining, the workers finally managed to move it some distance. Then the rock stopped and for two days would not move. Otomí reinforcements were called in to help. "As they began to pull it with many yells and whistles, the stone spoke: 'O wretched people, O unfortunate ones! Why do you persist in your desire to take me to the city of Mexico? Behold your work is in vain, since it is not my will to go there. But as you wish it this way, pull me and I will go as far as I wish, but it will be to your harm!'" Thereupon the rock allowed itself to be pulled with ease to a bridge just outside Tenochtitlan. At the bridge, it broke all the beams and fell into the water, wounding and drowning many men with it. Later, divers searched for the rock in the lake bed but could not find it anywhere. The rock had returned to its original place, where the Aztecs then found it "all covered with paper [offerings] and with signs of the sacrifices that it had been offered."

The Aztec emperor may have been the master of all the people in his realm, but no Aztec was the master of nature. The natural and supernatural worlds, which we ourselves separate, were one and the same to the Aztecs, who knew that no human could defy such forces. The Aztec people recognized that they were just one part within this vastly larger system, and their lot was to live and work within it. What set the Aztecs apart from their neighbors and enemies is the responsibility they felt for preserving this system.

THE BEGINNING

The world began in the place of duality, as the wisemen recalled it from their painted books. Ometecuhtli (Lord of Duality) and Omecihuatl (Lady of Duality), the primordial couple, gave birth to four strong sons, the four

Tezcatlipocas. The sons were the Red Tezcatlipoca, whose name was Xipe Totec (Our Lord the Flayed One); the Black Tezcatlipoca, whose name was Tezcatlipoca (Smoking Mirror); the White Tezcatlipoca, whose name was Quetzalcoatl (Feathered Serpent); and the Blue Tezcatlipoca, whose name was Huitzilopochtli (Hummingbird of the South). Each of the sons took a cardinal direction as his post, from which he would oversee all that happened and at which point, as a great tree, he and his brothers would support the heavens. The earth floated like an enormous crocodile on the primordial sea.

Two of the sons, Quetzalcoatl and Tezcatlipoca, had the task of separating the earth and sky. Tlaltecuhtli (Earth Lord) lay as a monstrous creature with snapping faces at all her joints. The brothers transformed themselves into great serpents; they descended and grabbed the earth monster at opposite ends, squeezed with all their might, and rent her asunder. They raised half of her to become the heavens; half they left below. The legend tells how the other gods then came to console Tlaltecuhtli's tattered remains; "they promised that from her would come all the vegetation necessary for human life." They formed from her body the surface of the earth. Her hair became the tall grasses, flowers, and trees; her skin became the short grasses and low-lying flowers; her eyes became wells, springs, and small caves; her mouth, the rivers and large caves; her nose, the valleys and mountains. Once formed, the earth "cried out in the night for the hearts of humans to eat; she would not be silent unless she was given these [hearts], and she would not bear fruit unless she was watered with human blood." She remained a voraciously hungry earth.

The painted books and the alphabetic texts derived from them also tell how the gods tried to bring human life to this world. Four times they tried, and four times their suns, or ages, met with disaster. The fifth time they succeeded. This fifth time is our time, and it, too, will end. The story, which has come down to us in many versions, is the Legend of the Suns.

Tezcatlipoca created the first age, when giants lived on the earth, subsisting on acorns. After many years, jaguars came to destroy this age and devour humankind. This happened in the year 4 Jaguar, which became the name of that sun.

Quetzalcoatl created the second age, during which humans lived on piñon nuts. Hurricanes and great winds swept away that age, and all humans were transformed into monkeys. The year of destruction was 4 Wind, the name of the age.

Tlaloc, the rain god, presided over the third age, when humans ate only the seeds of aquatic grasses. A fiery rain brought destruction; humans were turned into turkeys. The year this age ended was 4 Rain.

Chalchiuhtlicue, the goddess of ground water, created and destroyed the fourth age, a time when humans lived on wild seeds (an ancestral version of corn). The water goddess brought a great flood to end the age, and humans were transformed into fish. The year was 4 Water.

Tonatiuh, the sun god, presides over the fifth and present age, when humans subsist on corn. According to the legend, it is under this sun that there will occur earthquakes and hunger; and then the end of the world will come. This age will be destroyed by earthquakes, when the *Tzitzimime*, or celestial demons, will descend to devour humankind. The name of this sun is 4 Movement.

The Legend of the Suns was told over and over again, with variations as always, so that every Aztec knew it well. They lived in fear that they would see the end of the age. Stone monuments to the four previous ages were set around the ritual precinct of Tenochtitlan, as were monuments that showed all five. A monumental celebration of the Fifth Age is the Stone of the Sun, which most people know as the Aztec Calendar Stone.

With the destruction of the fourth sun and the opening of the fifth, the world and its features had to be reconstituted. Other legends told how this happened and how the present world of the Aztecs came to be. Father Sahagún wrote down the version told him by the sons of the old rulers: "It is told that when yet [all] was in darkness, when yet no sun had shone and no dawn had broken—it is said—the gods gathered themselves together and took counsel among themselves there at Teotihuacan. They spoke; they said among themselves: 'Come hither, O gods! Who will carry the burden? Who will take it upon himself to be the sun, to bring the dawn?'"

A fine and wealthy deity, Tecuciztecatl, presented himself: "O gods, I shall be the one." They needed a second volunteer, but no one else dared to come forward; everyone was afraid. Then the gods turned to poor deformed Nanahuatzin, who was covered with sores: "You be the one who is to give light, little pustule-covered one." He willingly obeyed. The gods raised a mountain for each one (the Pyramid of the Sun and the Pyramid of the Moon at Teotihuacan), where the two went to fast and perform penance for four days. Tecuciztecatl made costly offerings of precious feathers, balls of gold, and spines of red coral. Poor Nanahuatzin offered bundles of green rushes; he offered balls of straw and maguey spines which he reddened with his own blood.

When midnight came, the gods gathered in the Turquoise Enclosure around the bonfire that had burned for four days. Tecuciztecatl emerged in fine costume, Nanahuatzin clothed only in paper. The gods urged Tecuciztecatl to jump into the fire: "'Take courage, O Tecuciztecatl; fall—cast thyself—into the fire!' [But] the flames flared up high [and] he went terrified, stopped in fear, turned about, and went back." Four times he tried and failed. Then "Nanahuatzin, daring all at once, ...had no fear...; he quickly threw and cast himself into the fire.... Thereupon he burned; his body crackled and sizzled."

Taking heart from this brave action, Tecuciztecatl, too, cast himself in the fire. The story says that an eagle then came suddenly and threw itself into the

The Aztecs believed that the gods had created and destroyed the world on four separate occasions by means of floods, winds, and other disasters. Only on the fifth attempt, when a courageous god hurled himself into the sacrificial fire, and was resurrected as the Fifth Sun, did the world as they knew it evolve. The coronation stone of Moctezuma the Younger depicts this evolution. In the corners are the glyphs of the previous ages, surrounding the central glyph (4 Movement) of the present age.

flames, and afterwards a jaguar. The eagle's feathers were blackened and singed, and the jaguar's coat became spotted with soot; because of this daring, the valiant warriors are called the eagles and jaguars.

The next morning, the dawn reddened and glowed. In the east rose Nanahuatzin, the sun, brilliant, shining, blinding everything with its light. Then rose Tecuciztecatl, the moon, just behind, a little later, but shining with the same intensity. The gods said: "How can this be...? Will they perchance both together follow this same path? Will they both shine like this?" Then one of the gods came out running and threw a rabbit in the face of moon. He darkened Tecuciztecatl's face and deadened the moon's brilliance, such as it appears today. And so the Aztecs recognized a rabbit in the face of the moon.

The sun and the moon appeared over the earth together, but they could not move nor follow their paths. "So once again the gods spoke: 'How shall we live? The sun cannot move. ... [Let] this be, that through us the sun may be revived. Let all of us die.'" Thereupon the gods all gave themselves in sacrifice so that the sun and then the moon might move.

Thus the fifth sun, the present sun, was created through the sacrifice of the gods. First, Nanahuatzin boldly offered himself on the fire in order to become the sun; then, all the other deities gave their own lives to set it moving on its course. Just as the gods had surrendered their hearts to the sacrificial blade, the Aztecs believed humans must give their hearts to keep the sun and moon in motion. It became their mission as a chosen people to give the sun strength to fight its way across the heavens each day, and to battle its way across the underworld each night. It was their mission, too, to satisfy the earth's hunger for human hearts and thereby give her the strength to bear fruit. This sense of divine mission was at the core of Aztec religious zeal.

Even humankind itself was created with the blood of the gods. Several of the stories about the creation of the first humans feature Quetzalcoatl, who, along with Tezcatlipoca, had already separated the heavens from the earth. Human life had to originate with the bones of those who had lived in the fourth age, so Quetzalcoatl undertook the dangerous journey into Mictlan, the Underworld, a dark, cold place where those who died went for eternity. There he received the bones from Mictlantecuhtli, Lord of the Underworld. The route back from the underworld was arduous and danger-filled. Just as he was emerging, Quetzalcoatl fell and dropped the bones; they scattered and broke. The Aztec elders would say this is why humans are of different sizes: some short, some tall. Finally, Quetzalcoatl made his way back to Tamoanchan, Place of Origin, where the gods were assembled. An old goddess ground the bones like cornmeal. Then Quetzalcoatl and the other gods drew blood from their own bodies to wet the meal into a dough from which the first man and first women were formed. The bones of the ancestors and the blood of the gods made the first humans of this fifth age.

The humans were born into an ordered world. The earth spread out around them in four quarters, each guarded by a deity or a pair of gods and each with a cosmic tree that supported the heaven in that corner. In a Pre-Columbian pictorial almanac (the *Codex Féjérváry-Mayer*), the plain of the earth is presented as a Maltese cross, the four arms of the cross forming the cardinal directions. Each direction is pictured with its sacred tree, the bird associated with it, and two deities who preside over that direction; each direction has its own color. In the center, Xiuhtecuhtli, Lord of Fire, receives sacrificial blood from the corners. It is the picture of a world in balance.

The world was layered. Rising from the surface of the earth was a 13-layered heaven, where the sun and moon traveled, where comets appeared, and where

The first page of the *Codex Féjérváry-Mayer* shows the world in balance. The central panel contains **Xiuhtecuhtli** (god of fire and patron of the yearly cycle). **East**, where the sun-disk rises, is painted at the top; **West**, the place of women, where the sun sets, is at the bottom. Between them are portrayed **South**, on the right, and **North**, on the left.

the celestial deities were found. Extending below the earth's surface, the nine levels of the underworld stretched down. There the sun had to trespass each night, and there the dead remained forever in a cold stillness.

THE PATH OF TIME

Time began to run early in the creation process. One legend places the beginning of the calendar before the earth and sky were separated. Time was not so much created as it was discovered. The first part of the calendar to appear was the 20-day period, a count based on the number of fingers and toes humans have. In many Mesoamerican languages, although not in Nahuatl, the name of the 20-day period is a homonym of "human." A legend preserved from Guatemala, called "the birth of the 20-day period," tells how at the very beginning "it [meaning time] began to run, by itself, alone." The story relates how the people saw a human on the road, "but no human occurred;" they went to the road and wondered, "Who is it that passed by here now? Here are his tracks, right here. Measure them with your foot." There had been no human, however. What had passed was the 20-day count.

THE AZTEC DAY-COUNT

The fundamental Aztec calendar was the 260-day cycle, called the *tonalpohualli*, simply the "count of days." Twenty day signs ran consecutively, from Crocodile through Flower, repeating after the 20th day. Beside the day signs ran 13 day numbers, 1 through 13, the numbers advancing with each day up to 13, when they repeated again with 1. Thus, the day-count began with 1 Crocodile, 2 Wind, 3 House, 4 Lizard, and continued up to 13 Reed, when the numbers began again with 1: 1 Jaguar, 2 Eagle, 3 Vulture, and so forth. The 20 day signs and the 13 numbers, advancing side by side, yielded 260 uniquely named days. Often, this is presented by modern writers as two meshing cogs. But the Aztecs did not think in terms of wheels and did not use cogs. A better metaphor from their point of view would be two relay teams walking along at the same pace: one team has 20 walkers taking their turns and the other team has 13 walkers, who take their turns more frequently. Of the two components, it is the day signs that carry the most divinatory significance.

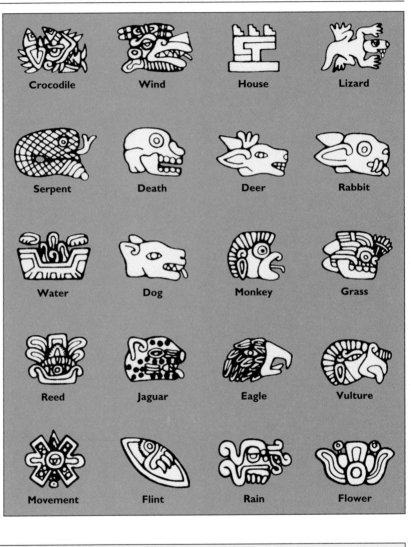

Crocodile   Wind   House   Lizard

Serpent   Death   Deer   Rabbit

Water   Dog   Monkey   Grass

Reed   Jaguar   Eagle   Vulture

Movement   Flint   Rain   Flower

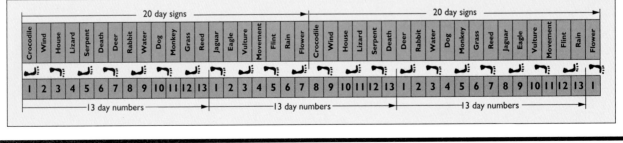

The 20-day count was the fundamental count, which repeated endlessly. Each of the 20 days had its symbol and name. The days were: Crocodile, Wind, House, Lizard, Serpent, Death, Deer, Rabbit, Water, Dog, Monkey, Grass, Reed, Jaguar, Eagle, Vulture, Movement, Flint (Knife), Rain, and Flower. After these finished, the 20 day-signs came around again. Each of these days also had a number, from 1 through 13, which also repeated. In this way, the day 1 Crocodile was followed by 2 Wind, 3 House, 4 Lizard, 5 Serpent, and so forth until the numbers arrived at 13 with 13 Reed, when 1 would occur again: 1 Jaguar, 2 Eagle, and so forth. The combination of 20 signs with 13 numbers formed a sacred count of 260 uniquely named days, a unit of time close to the period of human gestation. The Aztecs called it the *tonalpohualli*, simply the "day count," and it was the only count that truly mattered to them. Each of the day signs and each of the day numbers carried meaning for the Aztecs; gods, colors, directions, and rituals associated with each of these signs and numbers indicated what kind of day it would be. When the Aztecs named the days, this was the count they used.

Another calendar, tied to the solar year, operated at the same time. It functioned primarily to establish general planting and harvesting times, and to organize the solar year into a series of feasts. This 365-day year was divided into 18 "months" of 20 days each, with 5 unlucky and useless days remaining at the end. Each month had its own festival and took the name of that celebration. The individual days of these months were not themselves named, except if it were important to say that something happened on the eighth day of the first month of Atlcahualo, for example. Instead, the days always bore their tonalpohualli names. The Aztec chronicles record that Tenochtitlan was destroyed on the day 1 Serpent; it was only later that historians equated this day with the second day of the 10th month of Xocotlhuetzi.

The day count of 260 days and the solar year of 365 days meshed perfectly every 52 years and thereby created a 52-year cycle. This was the larger cycle by which historical events were measured. The years, each named according to the tonalpohualli day on which it ended, bore one of four signs (Rabbit, Reed, Flint, and House) and one of 13 numbers (1-13). Just as the tonalpohualli days progressed from sign to sign and from number to number, so did the years: 1 Rabbit preceded 2 Reed, 3 Flint, 4 House, 5 Rabbit, 6 Reed, and so forth. The signs and numbers of these years, like those of the days, carried their own augural meanings. 1 Flint, as we know, was a year for great beginnings, 1 Rabbit a year of drought and famine. The 52-year cycle functioned for the Aztecs somewhat like our century does for us, except that the Aztec cycle was shorter by almost half. We think of the beginning of centuries as times of birth or renewal, and during the century we reflect on those things that occurred 100 years before. So too, did the Aztecs. They understood that events that had occurred in previous cycles would affect the present, 52 years later. They considered the 52-year cycle as a

The ceremonial lighting of the New Fire on the chest of a specially chosen captive marked the beginning of a new 52-year cycle. The fire was quickly carried to the ritual precinct in Tenochtitlan. The *Codex Borbonicus* depicts the moment when priests from other temples lit their great torches from the New Fire in Huitzilopochtli's temple. Once the fire was fully ignited and visible to the people, there was great rejoicing. The Aztecs believed that if the New Fire could not be lit, the world would fall into darkness, and chaos, and demons would descend to devour humankind. Pregnant women were hidden in granaries during this time, and some individuals wore maguey-leaf masks to protect themselves.

metaphor for completion. Persons who had lived 52 years were considered old and retired; they had seen their cycle.

The completion of a 52-year cycle was a time of profound apprehension. It was a time when life paused and had to begin afresh; all the fires in the land were extinguished, to be kindled anew. The Aztecs understood that if this renewal did not occur, the world would be plunged into chaos and the Fifth Age would end. The renewal, called the Binding of the Years, occurred at the onset of the year 2 Reed. It was then that the 52 reeds of the years would be bound and buried and a new cycle started. Imperial sculptors carved replicas of 52 bound reeds to symbolize the completed and bound years; these were ceremoniously buried within altars in the ritual precinct.

Everyone was involved in the preparations for the closing of the cycle. As Father Sahagún's informants told him, "First they put out fires everywhere in the country round. And the statues, hewn in either wood or stone, kept in each man's home and regarded as gods, were all cast into the water." Cooking implements were thrown out, "and everywhere there was much sweeping—there was sweeping very clean. Rubbish was thrown out...." At night, the populace gathered on their housetops to wait in the darkness for the new fire to be kindled. Pregnant women put on maguey-leaf masks and hid in granaries, for it was believed that if the new fire were not drawn, the women "would be changed into fierce beasts" and "would eat men." The small children also wore maguey-leaf masks, and were kept awake so that they would not be turned into mice. The tension was high, because if the new fire could not be drawn, "then [the sun] would be destroyed forever; all would be ended; there would evermore be night," and the Tzitzimime, terrible demons of darkness, would descend to devour humankind.

The principal fire priests from Tenochtitlan had departed to a hilltop, the Hill of the Stars, in the southern valley. "At midnight, when the night divided in half," they drilled a new fire on the breast of a high-born captive. And "when [the fire] took flame, then speedily [the priest] slashed open the breast of the captive, seized his heart, and quickly cast it there into the fire. Thus he fed, he served it to the fire." Thus nourished, the fire "flared and burst into flames and was visible everywhere. It was seen from afar." All those waiting expectantly on the housetops then cut their ears and sprinkled their own blood in the direction of the new fire. The priests took the new fire directly to the Temple of Huitzilopochtli in Tenochtitlan, whence swift runners and strong warriors carried the fire to the other cities. From the principal temples, to the

The 52 years of a cycle, envisioned as 52 reeds, were bound together at the close of the cycle in the year 2 Reed. Stone replicas of these year bundles were ceremoniously deposited inside altars within the ritual precinct of Tenochtitlan. This stone bundle was carved to commemorate the New Fire ceremony of 1507—the last before the Spanish Conquest.

Chalchiuhtlicue, the goddess of ground-water—of springs and lakes—was a force of great importance to the Aztecs. As agriculturalists, they depended upon adequate and appropriately timed water, either from the ground or as rains. Most religious rituals centered on the gods of fertility and water. In the *Codex Borbonicus,* a mighty torrent of water flows from the image of Chalchiuhtlicue; before her lie bowls of offerings.

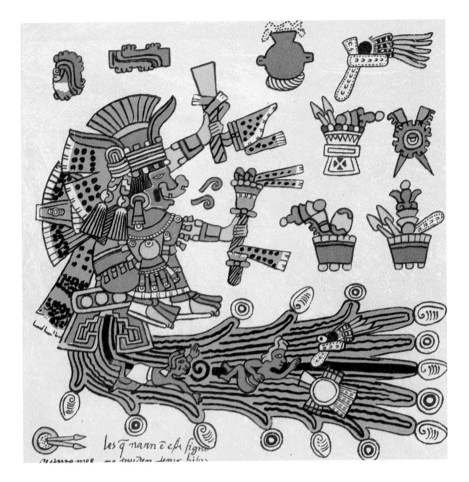

capulli temples, and then to the houses, the fire quickly spread. "There was the laying of many fires; there was the quieting of many hearts."

Then the households renewed themselves. All the people put on new clothes; they laid new mats and brought out new implements for the kitchen. "Then all rejoiced and there was feasting." The world had been preserved for another 52 years.

SACRALITY

Aztecs were close to their gods and worked with them in a reciprocal arrangement to ensure the wellbeing of humankind. As a group of Aztec elders and wisemen explained to the Spanish friars, "there is life because of the gods; with their sacrifice, they gave us life.... [The gods] provide our subsistence, all that we eat and drink, that which maintains life: corn, beans, amaranth, sage. To them do we petition for water, for rain which nourish things on earth."

The legends and the ancient stories speak of the Aztec deities as supernatural actors on a mythic stage, with roles to play and lives to give in sacrifice. This way of humanizing the supernatural has always been an effective narrative device, for it allows one to explain the cosmos in human terms that can readily be understood, and it worked well for the Aztec elders in stories of creation. It did not reflect the Aztecs' true view of their gods, however. Aztec gods were not divine humans, like Greek and Roman gods; they did not marry and have children; they did not feel emotions such as jealousy or competition; they did not reside on a cloud-draped mountaintop like the Greek gods did. The Aztec deities were not pagan gods in the sense that we usually think of them.

The closest word to "god" in Nahuatl is *teotl*, which the Spanish usually translated as "god," or sometimes "demon." Its real meaning, however, is spirit—a concentration of power as a sacred and impersonal force. In this way teotl is something close to the Polynesian conception of *mana*. The Aztec world was charged throughout with this energy, which could be manifest in rainstorms, springs, lakes, and even the deep-pitched sound of the great wooden barrel drum, the *huehuetl*. The Aztec deities were these sacred forces. Chalchiuhtlicue, the goddess of groundwater, was thus less a female supernatural than she was the power and force of the groundwaters themselves; she was the embodiment of the rivers and lakes. Father Sahagún's noble informants said that Chalchiuhtlicue "was the waters." Then the informants added that: "They represented her as a woman."

The "representation" of a deity was important to the Aztecs. The term they used was *teixiptla*, which can mean impersonator, image, and substitute. The teixiptla was the physical representation or incarnation of the teotl. This included the cult images of the gods, created in stone, wood, and amaranth seed dough, which sat in the temples or were paraded around during rituals; it included the assemblages of ritual costume that were composed on wood armatures to represent the deity at feasts; and it included the humans who represented or impersonated the gods during ceremonies. The sacrality of the teotl was called forth by and through its teixiptla. For the feast day of Chalchiuhtlicue, the priests "formed her image over a framework of wood," costumed it, and made offerings to it as a manifestation of the forces of groundwater. They connected with the teotl by virtue of the ritual.

Sacrality was also held in sacred bundles. Bundles that contained the ritual paraphernalia of a specific cult or of a people were among the most sacred objects the Aztecs had. The actual contents of the bundles might seem banal—corn, feathers, rubber, precious stones perhaps, wrapped up in cloth and leather—but each item referred to an area of sacrality or an episode of grave importance. Each cult had its sacred bundle that contained teotl. So, too, each altepetl had a sacred bundle pertaining to its patron deity, which the people had carried and guarded since their origin; these town bundles were called "the heart of the altepetl," because they contained the creative energy of the town. A descendant of the Texcocan royal house

The ruins of a shrine to Tlaloc, the Aztec god of rain, lie on the summit of Mount Tlaloc, on the eastern side of the Valley of Mexico. The temple was a sacred and ceremonial destination for Aztec kings—a meeting place between land and sky. Each year, during the dry season, the kings would lead a lavish procession across the valley and up the mountain to conduct ceremonies designed to ensure the coming of rain.

Tlaloc was a deity of supreme importance to a people whose lives depended on what they grew on the land. Farmers invoked him to send rains for their crops at the right times, to temper damaging storms, and to stay the killing frosts. The Aztecs considered his abode to be in the mountains, where the rain clouds formed. To him, they offered the most precious sacrifice—children. The Tlaloc effigy vessel on the opposite page was excavated from the Templo Mayor.

recalled how his ancestors had brought the sacred bundles of their gods with them to Texcoco. The Aztec migration stories picture or mention Huitzilopochtli's sacred bundle, which the Aztecs carried on their long journey from Aztlan. Thereafter it was kept in Huitzilopochtli's temple until the Conquest, when, according to Spanish records, the priests spirited it away just before the conquerors set fire to the temple. It was critical to save Huitzilopochtli's bundle, because the statues were teixiptla that could be replaced, but the bundle contained the teotl itself. Sacred energy was the bundle's content.

Aztec deities were this concentrated energy, manifest in anthropomorphic form as gods and goddesses. They pertained to slightly different but largely overlapping realms: storms and water, earth and agriculture, the sun and warfare, human fertility, and the like. We know these gods by name, but the forces they represented coincide so much with those of other gods that it is impossible to say where one domain ended and another began.

Storms and rain were the realm of Tlaloc, the principal water god. He brought the rain needed for agriculture, but he also brought thunder and lightning, hail and snow. He and the Tlaloque, the little mountain deities, were thought to dwell in the mountains, where the rain-bringing clouds formed. Tlaloc, whose name means earth, was the Aztec manifestation of the ancient Mesoamerican storm god, identifiable since Pre-Classic times by his fanged mouth and goggle eyes. Chalchiuhtlicue (Jades Her Skirt) was his watery counterpart on earth. She represented the groundwater of springs, rivers, and lakes. Both deities had costumes of turquoise blue, blue

jewels, and rubber-splattered paper offerings. Together with the deities of earth and agriculture, they promoted crop fertility and growth.

Tlaltecuhtli (Earth Lord), depicted as a monstrous crouching creature, embodied the earth, but the corn crop that grew from its topsoil was the purview of a series of corn deities: Xilonen (Young Corn Ear), who guarded the still-green corn; the principal corn goddess, Chicomecoatl (Seven Serpent); and a male deity, Centeotl (Maize Cob Lord). The Aztecs thought of the heart of the earth as a jaguar, which they deified as Tepeyollotl (Heart of the Earth). Mictlantecuhtli, who presided over the Underworld, was visualized as a skeleton.

A group of male deities represented the celestial sphere and the battlefield that fed the sun. The sun itself was personified as Tonatiuh (Sun), although the ritual and rhetoric of the Aztec Templo Mayor was increasingly equating the sun with Huitzilopochtli, the Aztec patron deity. Huitzilopochtli was the Aztecs' principal god of war, the prototype of the valiant Aztec warrior who himself slew all his enemies. His Tlaxcalan counterpart, as war god, was Mixcoatl (Cloud Serpent), the hunting god and patron deity of the Tlaxcala. Another force for battle was the planet Venus, believed to kill the sun with its rays when it rose as the evening star; it was personified as Tlahuizcalpantecuhtli (Dawn Lord). A legend tells how a female deity, Itzpapalotl (Obsidian Butterfly), was the first to die in war.

A cluster of female deities presided over human fertility and generally merged with the earth lord as wide-ranging forces. Toci (Our Grandmother), also called Teoinnan (Mother of the Gods), was patroness of curers and midwives. Cihuacoatl (Serpent Woman), Coatlicue (Serpents Her Skirt), and Tonantzin (Our Mother) were all earth and fertility incarnations. Human lust and pleasure were embodied in Xochiquetzal (Flower Feather), while licentiousness and childbirth both were the realm of Tlazolteotl (Filth Deity), who was the patroness of weavers. Mayahuel and the many pulque gods were all deities of fertility as well as pulque.

Quetzalcoatl (Feathered Serpent) and Tezcatlipoca (Smoking Mirror) stand out. These two, described as brothers who separated heaven from earth and as opposing forces at ancient Tula, were often juxtaposed in Aztec thought. Tezcatlipoca, the dark force, could be malevolent, although he was also the patron of rulers and the god of divination. Quetzalcoatl, the light force, was considered beneficial; he brought back the ancestral bones of which the first humans were formed; he brought knowledge to humankind; and he was also patron of the priests. As Ehecatl (Wind), he blew the wind from a trumpet-like mouth mask. As Venus, he was both the morning and the evening star.

All the altepetl, capulli, and occupational groups had their patron deities, to which they paid special attention. We have already seen how Huitzilopochtli drove the Mexica, and how Cihuacoatl fought for the

Mictlantecuhtli was the lord of the underworld and custodian of the bones of the dead. On this carved marble tumbler, uncovered during the Templo Mayor excavations, Mictlantecuhtli is depicted wearing a feather crown, a necklace of human hearts, and long cloth earrings that refer to death and the underworld. His eyes bulge out through the sockets of his skull.

Xochimilca; Tezcatlipoca was patron god of the Texcoca, and Mixcoatl looked after the Tlaxcala. Within the altepetl, the capulli also had their own patrons, as did the artisans. The weavers looked to Tlazolteotl to guide their art, the painters to Xochiquetzal, and the goldsmiths to Xipe Totec (Our Lord the Flayed One). The merchants asked Yacatecuhtli (Nose Lord) to watch over their journeys and receive their offerings. These groups, like the capulli and altepetl, were all attached to supernatural entities from whom they gained energy.

No part of the Aztec world lay outside the realm of the sacred.

Ritual conversation with the supernatural and natural worlds continues to be important to rural life in Mexico, where elements of old Aztec rites light vigil that takes place each November on the Day of the Dead, a Catholic feast with strong roots in rural Spain, has absorbed traces of the

endure in some Catholic ceremonies. The candle-
Aztecs' Great Feast of the Dead.

7

A WORLD IN BALANCE

In both the spectacles of public temples and the privacy of their own homes, Aztecs invoked the sacred forces and made offerings to them on a regular basis. Ritual, supplication, and thanksgiving were an integral part of the daily routine. The priests in the ritual precincts seemed always to be active on behalf of the populace; they shouldered most of the responsibility for attending to the supernatural forces. But the common people, too, knew they had obligations to the gods.

Each house had its shrine, with a few simply made cult figures, where offerings were given, supplications brought, and debts to the gods promised and paid. Women might petition the fertility goddesses for a child. The farmer might invoke the rain god; arriving at his fields, he would address the rain, the corn, the earth, and the sun. The fisherman out on the lake would appeal to the groundwater goddess. A small ritual at a crossroads shrine might help the traveler pass unharmed. Many times there were simple acts of communication and mediation. For example, Father Sahagún records that when women put dried corn in the cooking pot, "first of all they breathed upon [the corn]. ... In this way it would not take fright; thus it would not fear the heat." In such personal ways, the Aztecs constantly sought to soothe the energies around them.

On both small and large scales, the Aztecs did what they could to keep an ordered and balanced world. Individually, they tried to live prudently and modestly to achieve harmony with the myriad forces that affected their lives. As for dealing with the broader world in its cosmic vastness, they relied on their priests to perform the appropriate ceremonies that would insure stability and continuation.

ATTENDING TO TIME

It was not just nature that was alive with sacrality. Time, too, carried forces and energies that had to be understood and taken into consideration. Each day was spiritually different from the day before it and the day following it, and from all other of the 260 days in the *tonalpohualli*. Each of the 20 day symbols carried its own augural associations; the 13 numbers likewise had theirs. Together, the symbol and number combinations contributed to the quality of each day, making it unique. Some days were auspicious for certain kinds of activities, and some were not. Some days foretold a good fate, and others equivocated.

The auspices and associations carried by various units of time were recorded in painted almanacs, called *tonalamatls*, or books of the day. The day keepers, who were soothsayers and wisemen, read the tonalamatls and interpreted their painted messages. Fortunately, several ancient Aztec tonalamatls have come down to us. They show how the system worked. Each of the day symbols had layered associations, beginning first with the meaning of the symbol itself and then with other gods or sacred elements that might be attached to it. Each of the numbers had its elements, too. Thirteen augural birds and 13 Lords of the Day accompanied the 13 numbers. In addition, there were 9 Lords of the Night, who influenced the days in rotation. Then, patron gods would govern periods of 13 days. Larger blocks of time—52-day periods and 65-day periods—carried additional associations.

This rich layering of forces can be seen in the sacred almanac of the *Codex Borbonicus*, each page of which pertains to a 13-day period when one or two deities preside. For the fourteenth period, for example, the patron gods are Xipe Totec (wearing his characteristic flayed skin) and the feathered serpent

The *tonalamatl*, an almanac painted on bark paper, recorded the fates and forces associated with the 260-day *tonalpohualli*, the Aztec day count. The tonalamatl of the *Codex Borbonicus* is divided into 20 "weeks" of 13 days each; the Spaniards called these periods *trecenas*. Each page of the almanac focuses on a separate trecena. Shown here is Trecena 14, which was governed by the deities Xipe Totec and the feathered serpent Quetzalcoatl, who appear in the large panel. Below and to the right are the 13 days, which are identified by their symbols and the numbers 1 to 13; one of the 9 Lords of the Night accompanies each day. The 13 Lords of the Day and the 13 augural birds appear in adjacent compartments.

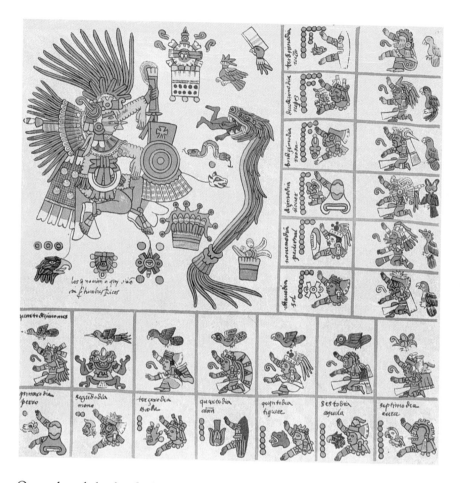

Quetzalcoatl, both of whom are painted in the main panel, surrounded by ritual paraphernalia and abbreviated images of ceremonies. The individual days and their companions are painted in rectangular compartments below and to the right of the patrons. Beginning in the lower left box, the days of this period start with 1 Dog, and continue to the right: 2 Monkey, 3 Grass, 4 Reed, 5 Jaguar, 6 Eagle, and 7 Vulture. Then the days continue from bottom to top: 8 Movement to 13 Wind. In the same box as each day is one of the nine Lords of the Night who influences that day. These lords are depicted only from the waist up, with their arms outstretched in front of them in the gesture of sacred control. The other boxes hold the 13 Lords of the Day and the 13 augural birds, each pertaining to one of the 13 day numbers. The influences represented by these signs, symbols, and deities combine to form the meaning and energy contained in each day.

As soon as a child was born, the parents sought to know his or her fate, for a person's fate was governed by the day on which he or she was born and the day on which he or she was named. As Father Sahagún recorded:

According to tradition, a child's fate was governed by the day on which he or she was born. The parents of a newborn would summon a soothsayer, or day keeper, on the day of birth to name their child, but if he felt the day did not augur well, he would recommend waiting for a more favorable day. The illustration below, taken from the *Florentine Codex*, shows a day keeper reading the augury for an infant born on 10 Rabbit.

And when the baby was born, then they read the day signs. They summoned the soothsayer [literally, the day-count reader]; they told him the instant it had arrived, the instant it had been born. Then he opened out, he looked at their books, at his paintings, his writings; he read, examined, looked at the day sign on which the baby was born, studied which were those related to it which governed there. If perhaps it was a bad day, perhaps good were its companions which governed there. This improved it.

If the day of birth was baleful, the day keeper suggested that the parents wait for a favorable day on which to name the child. The child would carry his birthday and name-day auguries with him throughout his life.

The Aztec divinatory system resembled modern astrology, except that augural meaning for the Aztecs was contained in the day signs and numbers rather than in the relative position of heavenly bodies. The Aztecs certainly watched the stars, planets, and various constellations, but they did not codify a zodiac and build a divinatory system around it. Instead, their divinatory system grew directly from the 260-day ritual calendar.

A person's birthday governed his fate for better or for worse. The day 1 Deer, for example, bode well. Sahagún said: "He who was then born a nobleman, who was of noble lineage, became a ruler and gained fame.... And if it were only a commoner who was then born, the same likewise befell him. He attained his ends; he succeeded. He lived. He became a brave warrior, a valiant chieftain. He surpassed others." This was the birthday of Nezahualcoyotl, the Texcocan ruler who, as a youth, lived in exile until he and Itzcoatl could overthrow Tezozomoc, the lord of Azcapotzalco. Nezahualcoyotl, the most esteemed of all Texcocan rulers, fulfilled his birth prognostication despite great hardships.

Other signs could be less favorable. The next day, 2 Rabbit, the day of the pulque gods, meant that the child would grow up to be a drunkard. The day 3 Water was mixed: "For he who was born on it, so it was said, would prosper. All his wealth would come easily.... But, on the other hand, quickly would vanish that which had come to him. Like water it would pass away—as if carried off by the river; as if engulfed by the water." The day 4 Dog brought lasting prosperity to a person, especially if he chose to breed dogs for food: his dogs would all mate and multiply; none would sicken and die. "It was said: 'How can it be otherwise? The dogs share a day sign with him.'"

The qualities of the days thus carried over to the person. The day 5 Monkey gave the ability to tell tales, to jest, and to amuse others; it meant one would be universally liked. A wild sign, 6 Grass, brought torment and pain. "Rugged day signs" made one brave. One could improve one's fate with careful living and attention to proper penance. Still, the qualities of one's day would continue to exert their influence.

Even an individual born under the most auspicious day sign, however, could meet disaster if he or she forgot to heed the day signs. The days carried meaning for every activity, and, in the Aztec world, it was crucial that events happen at the right time. Merchants knew that they should only begin their journeys on a few favorable days: 1 Crocodile, 1 Monkey, 7 Serpent, or, the best, 1 Serpent, called "the straight way." Approaching home, they would delay on the route to wait for a good day sign for the homecoming. Father Durán was amazed that the Aztecs followed the signs of the days rather than the signs of the fields when it came time to harvest. He recalled how the people would not harvest their corn, even though it was ready and in danger of rotting, until the correct day had arrived: "They could have gathered the crop earlier, at their leisure; but since the old sorcerer found in his book or almanac that the day had come, he proclaimed it to the people, and they went off in great speed." Father Durán clearly did not understand that timing—doing things according to the auguries of the days—was fundamental to maintaining a balanced world.

LIVING CORRECTLY

The Aztecs learned how to maintain the world in balance. This wisdom came from their ancestors, the "forefathers, the old men, the old women, the white-haired ones" who left them guidelines by which to live. After the Conquest, a group of Aztec lords defended their traditions before the newly arrived Spanish friars by saying that their ancestors taught them their customs and beliefs. "From them we have inherited our pattern of life which in truth did they hold.... They taught us all their rules of worship, all their ways of honoring the gods. Thus before them [the gods] we prostrate ourselves; in their names we bleed ourselves; our oaths we keep, incense we burn, and sacrifices we offer." So it was recorded in the *Colloquies of the Twelve*.

It was the duty of the *tlamatinime*, the wisemen, as well as the elders, to keep these ancestral traditions alive. As the Aztec lords patiently explained to the Spanish friars in 1524, the wisemen were "those who guide us; they govern us, they carry us on their back and instruct us how our gods must be worshipped; whose servants we are, like the tail and the wing; who make offerings, who burn incense, those who receive the title of Quetzalcoatl [priest]. The experts, the knowers of speeches and orations, it is their obligation; they busy themselves day and night with the placing of the incense, with their offering, with the thorns to draw their blood. Those who see, those who dedicate themselves to observing the movements and the orderly operations of the heavens, how the night is divided. Those who observe [read] the codices, those who recite [tell what they read]. Those who noisily turn the pages of the painted manuscripts. Those who have possession of the black and red ink [a metaphor for wisdom] and of that which is pictured; they lead us, they guide us, they tell us the way. Those who arrange how a year falls, how the counting of destinies, and days, and each of the twenty-day months all follow their courses. With this they busy themselves, to them it falls to speak of the gods." The wisemen were consistently described as the bearers of ancient tradition and the keepers of the words of the ancestors.

The painted manuscripts held much of this tradition. Because they contained the teachings of the ancestors, they were the guides for living. The wiseman was one "in whose hands lay the books, the paintings; who preserved the writings, who possessed the knowledge, the tradition, the wisdom which hath been uttered." An episode from the deep Aztec past, recorded by Father Sahagún, illustrates just how important the painted manuscripts were. During their long migration, a contingent of Aztecs wanted to remain at Tamoanchan, a mythic place of origin and bounty. Finally the principal priests and wisemen left them there and went on without them; they "carried the god on their backs ...wrapped in a bundle.... They carried the writings, the books, the paintings. They carried the knowledge; they carried all—the song books, the flutes." Four wisemen who remained behind with the rest bemoaned their fate, saying: "'How will the common people live, how will they dwell?... They carried away the writings.... How will the lands, the mountains be? How will all live? What will govern? What will rule? What will lead? What will show the way? What will be the model, the standard?'... Then they [the wisemen] devised the book of days, the book of years, the count of the years, the book of dreams. They arranged the reckoning just as it had been kept. And thus time was recorded." By painting the sacred books anew, the remaining wisemen recreated the models and standards for living.

This ancestral wisdom, preserved in the books, was circulated through ritual and by the prognostications of the day keepers. Largely, however, it was brought out in the formal speeches and orations called the *huehuetlatolli*, the "old-old" speeches or discourses of the elders that voiced the ancient religious and moral doctrines and advertised the rules by which people should live. Different orations were spoken at every major point in a person's life. At birth, coming of age, marriage, and death, the huehuetlatolli reminded the people how to live correctly. Young boys and girls going off to one of the schools heard the formal speeches about proper conduct. Elaborate and lengthy discourses accompanied the inauguration of a ruler.

The fundamental message conveyed in the huehuetlatolli was that all people should live prudently. A father, for example, counseled his son to comport himself well. The lad was not to sleep excessively, nor drink or eat immoderately, lest he choke or become a gluttonous spectacle. In traveling, he was to walk "peacefully, quietly, tranquilly, deliberately," not go jumping about like a fool, or waddling like a mouse, or shamelessly strutting. He was to clothe himself neither vainly nor in tatters, but to wear his good cape tied moderately over his shoulder. He was to speak slowly and distinctly, not to growl or squeak like a rustic. Nor was he to gossip. The father advised his son that the world was a difficult place; a son could easily become lost if he strayed from the guidelines established by the ancestors. "They [the ancestors] went saying that on earth we travel, we live along a mountain peak. Over here there is an abyss, over there is an abyss. Wherever thou art to deviate, wherever thou art to go astray, there wilt thou fall, there wilt thou plunge into the deep. This is to say it is necessary that thou always act with discretion."

Those who wandered from the moral way were quickly cast out of Aztec society. They could be physically banished from their altepetl and forced to wander in the wilds, for no other altepetl would take them in. Murderers were killed, unless they were placed in bondage to their victim's family. Thieves were made to repay what they stole by becoming slaves to their victims; repeat offenders were killed. If the victims did not want these offenders around them and did not desire their labor, they could sell the criminals to others. Adulterers were stoned to death in the marketplace. Dishonest judges and tax collectors were executed. Pipiltin, because of their exalted status, were held to a higher standard than the commoners. Thus, if a young macehualli became drunk, he was beaten with wooden staves, "but if he was a nobleman's son, they strangled him." Aztec justice was swift and generally unforgiving, for crimes were dangerous to a balanced world.

KEEPING THE BALANCE WITH HEARTS AND BLOOD

The Aztecs understood their world to be a fragile and tenuous organism. It was inherently unstable, precariously balanced for the present, but liable to fall out of kilter at any moment. If that happened on a grand scale, the world, like humans who strayed from the moral path, would plunge into a cosmic abyss. All would be destroyed; chaos would rule. Life would end, and emptiness and darkness would prevail. Physically, the cities would "choke with trees, fill with stones," and the temples would "fall to pieces," Sahagún reported. To a lesser peril, small imbalances occurred all the time. The rains did not come or came too much; frost destroyed the crops; the moon obscured the sun, and the stars appeared during the day. At all times the Aztecs were watchful of these small imbalances, and were mindful of the need to correct them.

The world not only required constant attention to keep it upright; it also had to be fueled. All parts of it were alive with sacred energy, and all parts ideally worked in step with each other. But they could easily lose momentum if they were not nourished. The earth required sustenance to be bountiful. The sun needed strength-giving food to battle the darkness and appear in the dawn, and then to journey across the sky each day. The waters, too, were

hungry. Without sustenance, these forces could slow. The earth's fields might become sterile, the sun might stall in the sky or not rise at all, and the waters might diminish and dry. The Aztecs could not neglect the natural or supernatural forces; they had to nurture and feed them.

These forces had all been created through the sacrifices of the gods. Nanahuatzin gave up his life to become the sun; then the gods offered themselves in sacrifice to set it on its course. The gods promised to sustain the voracious earth with hearts and blood. They even created humankind with blood drawn from their own flesh. Because the gods had created the world forces with their supernatural blood, the Aztecs understood that only human blood could sustain it. The Aztecs felt more than a straightforward obligation to the world around them; they considered themselves to be the people divinely ordained to maintain the cosmic system. It was their destiny to feed the supernatural forces, the gods, with human blood.

All the rites and offerings and sacrifices went toward this goal. Ceremonies were regularly accompanied by offerings of copal incense, food of various kinds and configurations, paper, liquid rubber (often spattered on papers), feathers and grasses, jewels and textiles, and the blood of animals and humans. The priests commonly sacrificed quail and other birds, and also offered serpents or small mammals. The gods, however, prized the blood of humans above all.

Bloodletting was a common practice throughout the land. From the time the young boys and girls entered the *calmecac* (the school for noble children), they learned to cut their earlobes, or to pierce their tongues to draw blood. On marked occasions throughout their lives, they would cut themselves with small obsidian knives or pierce themselves with maguey spines to give their blood ceremonially.

The rulers drew blood from themselves on great state occasions. The large relief plaque carved in the year 8 Reed (1487) to commemorate the dedication of the Templo Mayor pictures the deceased ruler Tizoc and his living successor Ahuitzotl drawing blood from their ears with bone awls; they had already pierced their thighs and arms. The blood from their ears flows into the open mouth of the earth, while bone bloodletters are stuck like pins in a great grass ball. At their inaugurations, of course, and throughout their careers, the rulers thus offered their blood to the gods.

The priests, above all others, gave their blood freely. Their ears were so regularly cut that they became shredded. In the painted books, the priests are pictured with a patch of red on the jaw in front of their ear, a spot from which they regularly drew blood. The bloodied bone and maguey spines were thrust into grass balls or laid out on fir branches as offerings. Never were they thrown away, according to Father Durán, who remarked that the Spanish friars were amazed at the quantity of used thorns that were carefully warehoused and honored in the temples.

Bloodletting and blood offerings were ancient traditions in Mesoamerica. In the lower part of this page from the *Codex Tudela*, two worshippers, who carry fringed, white incense pouches over their arms, pierce their tongue and ears, respectively, with large bone awls; to the right, a ball of copal burns above an offering of paper. The upper part of the page depicts a heart sacrifice before the altar of one of the earth or underworld deities, whose ferocious image clamors for more hearts and blood. As in this illustration, sacrificial priests are often portrayed with a coating of black body paint.

The knives that cut the living hearts from sacrificial victims bore elaborately carved handles, often embellished with rich mosaic work. Here, an eagle warrior straddles the handle of such a blade.

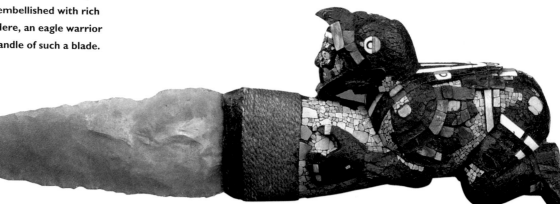

The male youth chosen to impersonate the god Tezcatlipoca for a year before being sacrificed had to be physically perfect. In this painting from the *Florentine Codex*, the young deity impersonator wears a quetzal-feathered headdress and holds Tezcatlipoca's feather shield and baton. Rulers and noble men and women pay him homage.

Dance and music were integral parts of Aztec ritual. The youth selected to impersonate Tezcatlipoca had to be able to play the flute well. As he prepared for his death by sacrifice, he would have played a flute much like these ceramic ones from the Templo Mayor.

The greatest offering was the heart of a living victim. These donors were either war captives, incorrigible slaves, or individuals chosen from the Aztec populace because of their special qualities. Regardless of their lives on earth, it was believed that when these people died on the sacrificial stone they became divine beings who would accompany the sun. The chronicles repeatedly stress that the victims went willingly to their fate. A war captive would have learned from birth that the most highly esteemed death he could face would be on the sacrificial stone, and his whole life was in preparation for such an end. At the time of his sacrifice, the warrior was called upon to "savor the fragrance, the sweetness of death by the obsidian knife." Thereafter, he would rejoice and forever live in abundance and happiness, like the hummingbird sucking the nectar of flowers.

For the feast to the god Tezcatlipoca, a male youth was selected from the available captives. Father Sahagún records that the boy was trained to impersonate the god for a year before being sacrificed. The chosen one had to be intelligent and physically perfect. He could be neither too thin nor too fat, neither too tall nor too short; he could have no blemish, no scar, no lump; his skin had to be smooth like a tomato's; his hair had to be long and straight. Great care was taken to teach him to play the flute and whistle. For a year he lived graciously and, esteemed as the god, was elegantly attired and in the company of lords and priests. He married and lived with four female deity impersonators until just before the feast. On the days of the feast, he sang and played his instruments through the city. Then, when he arrived at the temple where he was to die, "he ascended by himself, he went up of his own free will, to where he was to die." As he climbed, "he broke, he shattered his flute, his whistle."

Xipe Totec was the god of renewal and the patron god of goldworkers. To honor him, Xipe impersonators donned the flayed skin of a sacrificial victim. The stone statue at right, whose front and back are shown, illustrates how cords attached to such a skin secured it to the back of the head and body.

Çxxi de março dia desant
Benito. tlaca xi peualiztli
es gran fiesta

One of the many forms of Aztec ritual sacrifice, as shown here in an image from the *Codex Magliabechiano*, was a gladiatorial contest between a warrior clad in a jaguar skin and a war captive dressed as the deity Xipe Totec and tethered to a stone. The captive's club—his sole weapon against the warrior's deadly obsidian-bladed club—held only feathers.

Preceded and surrounded by elaborate ritual, by the smoke of incense and the sound of music and song, the sacrificial act was itself very quick. Father Durán described how the sacrificial victims were stretched on their backs over the bluntly pointed sacrificial stone. Four priests held the limbs in place. "The high priest then opened the chest and with amazing swiftness tore out the heart, ripping it out with his own hands. Still steaming, the heart was lifted toward the sun, and the fumes were offered up to the sun." Then the heart was placed in an "eagle vessel," a special receptacle for hearts, and the cult figures might be fed with the blood. The bodies of most of the victims were then rolled down the temple stairs, although Tezcatlipoca's impersonator was carefully carried down.

Different gods and different occasions called for variations in the ritual. For the second monthly feast, Tlacaxipehualiztli, which means the Flaying of Men, the deity Xipe Totec (Our Lord the Flayed One) was honored by the death of many deity impersonators. After the victims' hearts had been torn from their bodies, a priest would then flay the bodies, cutting the skin from the nape of the neck to the rump and peeling it away in one piece. Others donned the skins, taking up the garments and insignia of the deity impersonators to continue the impersonation. Also during this feast, warriors clad as eagles and jaguars did ritual battle against war captives who were tethered to a gladiatorial stone. The eagle and jaguar warriors were fully armed, but the captives' clubs held only feathers. Still, an exceptionally skilled—or lucky—captive, a particularly accomplished warrior, could do his adversary considerable harm before falling himself to the sounding of drums, trumpets, and flutes.

The feast and debt payment to the rain gods, during which children were sacrificed, was as poignant to the Aztecs as it remains to us. As Sahagún's informants recalled, on all the mountaintops around the valley, the priests set up long poles on which they hung sacrificial banners, paper streamers spotted with rubber. In seven locations they also "left children known as 'human paper streamers,' those who had two cowlicks of hair, whose day signs were favorable.... It was said: 'They are indeed the most precious debt-payments. [The Tlalocs] gladly receive them; they want them.'" The children were adorned with precious feathers and jade necklaces; they wore rubber sandals and were painted with liquid rubber; to the sound of flutes, they were carried on litters to their deaths. "There was much compassion. They made one weep;...they made one sad for them..." If the children cried, "if their tears kept flowing, if their tears kept falling, it was said, it was stated: 'It will surely rain.' Their tears signified rain."

Humans were the most valued gift the Aztecs could offer to the gods. Their hearts were "eagle cactus-fruits;" their blood was the "precious water" that sustained life; they became the "divine dead." Perhaps some 20,000 hearts were offered throughout the land each year; certainly, they were offered at every major ceremony and every monthly feast in the cities and towns alike. The Aztecs conceptualized sacrifice in ideological terms; they did not consider it otherwise.

It remains for us who do not share their world view to imagine the effect this quantity of sacrifice would have had on Aztec demographics. Some historians and anthropologists have argued that this ritual killing was a means of population control. I think this was not the case to any great extent. Most of the victims were warriors from hostile or newly won polities; their deaths would reduce the population of the distant provinces and might circumvent potential rebellion, but this would not have had much of an effect on the Valley of Mexico. The valley people were robbed of vigorous males when Aztec warriors died on foreign sacrificial stones and on distant battlefields, as they did in Axayacatl's disastrous Tarascan campaign. Such losses left many valley women widowed—an inevitable result of warfare—but the Aztecs were more often victorious than not. Many fewer Aztecs gave their hearts to the gods than died ordinary deaths of disease and old age. And so, as much as they might have wished it otherwise, fewer Aztecs became companions of the sun after death than endured in the underworld coldness of Mictlan.

The temple precinct dominates the island city of Tenochtitlan in this anonymously drawn map, published in Nuremberg in 1524 in a book

artist has placed the city at the center of Lake Texcoco, befitting Tenochtitlan's prestige as imperial capital. Causeways radiate out to smaller,

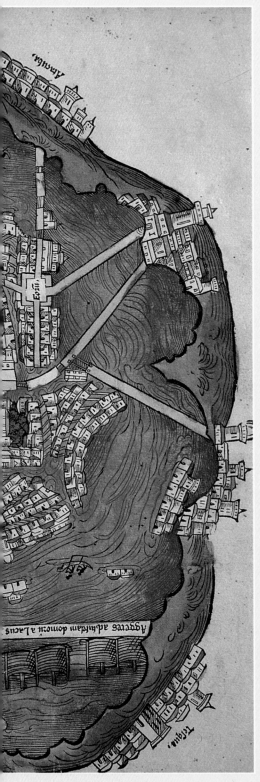

describing the exploits of Hernán Cortés. The subordinate cities on shore.

8

THE HEART OF THE EMPIRE

Tenochtitlan was the center of the Aztec world. Economically, it was the richest city in the land. Tribute poured into it from near and distant provinces. Great numbers of merchant caravans went forth and came home to the Tlatelolco marketplace, the largest market anyone had ever seen. Dense habitation on the island made it more populous than any of its neighboring settlements, and its concentration of *pipiltin* (nobles) drew artists and skilled specialists. Politically, it was where major decisions were made, where allied rulers traveled or resided in order to be near the center of power. It was from Tenochtitlan that imperial armies went out to war and returned with captives for the sacrificial stones. The Aztec gods had their greatest temples there, and there the most elaborate rituals were held. In every practical way, Tenochtitlan was the heart of the Aztec empire.

Tenochtitlan's features, history, and status additionally contributed to its conceptualization as the center of the cosmos, with the ritual precinct as world navel, or axis. The four barrios of the city, which radiated out from the precinct, were like the four quarters of the earth. The lake all around was like the waters that surround the earth. At its center, the towering Templo Mayor metaphorically linked the heavens with the earth and reached down to penetrate the levels of the underworld. The ritual precinct became the conduit for supernatural energy coming from the gods.

THE RITUAL PRECINCT

All the social, economic, and ideological elements of the empire came together at Tenochtitlan, with the Templo Mayor at its core. The people who stood, danced, or were sacrificed there never had any doubt that they were at the center of the universe. They had only to look around them at the arrangement of massive temple pyramids and wide plazas, and at the fearsome and monumental sculptures, to understand the importance and centrality of the place.

The Spaniards leveled the ritual precinct and the area around it during the Conquest, so that little trace remained on the surface. We know its features largely from the descriptions of the chroniclers and from two 16th-century plans, one made to accompany Cortés' second letter to Charles V (published in 1524) and one painted by Father Sahagún's noble informants decades later. Archaeological excavations in downtown Mexico City in this century have touched on a few of the temples. Building construction and renovation in the city have uncovered a great number of sculptures. Since 1978, when workers hit the monumental Coyolxauhqui stone, archaeologist Eduardo Matos Moctezuma and his team have concentrated on excavating the Templo Mayor itself, as well as the surrounding structures. The ritual heart of the Aztec empire, long known only through descriptions, lies uncovered at last.

What one sees today behind the Cathedral, just off the Zócalo, or main square, are the remains of earlier construction epochs, for the temple pyramid was enlarged and refurbished at least seven times in its history, and the later renovations suffered greatly from the shovels and sledgehammers of the Spaniards. Excavation exposed the layers of construction and renovation, like the layers of an onion, that made up the massive bulk of the pyramid Cortés and Moctezuma the Younger climbed together, although of that last construction phase itself there remains hardly anything. Today we see the Templo Mayor not as a finished, perfect product, but as a collection of fragments of a

The Templo Mayor, with its twin shrines to Tlaloc and Huitzilopochtli, towers above the sacred precinct in a model reconstruction housed in the National Museum of Anthropology in Mexico City. The structure to the left of the temple was a meeting place for members of the knightly orders. Facing the Templo Mayor is the round temple of Ehecatl-Quetzalcoatl. Behind this shrine is an enclosed ball court and a rectangular structure, or *tzompantli*, which held the skulls of sacrificial victims. The *calmecac* (school for noble children) occupies the foreground.

living thing that grew in grandeur as it changed over the years. Instead of a single statement, the Templo Mayor exists as phrases from an ancient oration that varied with each repeating.

In Moctezuma the Younger's time, a wall, cut by three monumental gates, separated the sacred space of the ritual precinct from the ordinary space beyond. At the center, the Templo Mayor rose as the largest temple pyramid in the precinct. Its facade looked west, so that those who climbed the two broad stairways to reach the twin temples ascended upward and eastward. The sun, on the day of its equinox, rose between the shrines. Monumental serpent heads at the foot of the staircases visually transformed the long balustrades into colossal serpents, their heads below and their bodies extending upwards on either side of the stairs. At the base of the pyramid were the heads of two enormous Fire Serpents, companions of the sun, that measured almost five feet (1.5 meters) in height, their long, upward-curling snouts punctuated with spherical stars. An undulating serpent wall delineated the pyramid's forecourt.

The excavation of the Templo Mayor uncovered the existence of at least five pyramids, stacked like nesting boxes. The temple pyramid was expanded several times, the oldest structure probably dating from the 1300s. The Spanish leveled the temple precinct, quarrying stone from its temples for their own buildings. As shown above, the excavated Templo Mayor reveals the bases or outlines of successive Aztec constructions.

At the top, the temple of Tlaloc stood on the north side and the temple of Huitzilopochtli on the south—his natural direction, as Hummingbird of the South. The interior walls were covered with murals and with carvings in relief. Like all Aztec temples, the shrines themselves were relatively small and fairly dark. They were large enough to hold the cult images and some ritual paraphernalia, but they never were intended to accommodate crowds. The pageantry and ritual all took place outside, in front of the temples, on the broad platforms at the summit of the pyramids, in the plazas, and along the processional ways. On either side of the temples, great stone men sat holding the banners of the cult. At the entrance to the Tlaloc temple, a stone altar carved as a reclining man in the configuration known as a *chacmool* received offerings to the rain god. At the bottom of the Tlaloc stairway, an altar of toads, harbingers of rain, jutted into the forecourt. Before the entrance to Huitzilopochtli's shrine, a sacrificial stone awaited victims. At the base of his stairway lay the great sculpture of the decapitated and dismembered Coyolxauhqui, his defeated sister.

During the excavation of the Templo Mayor, archaeologists discovered this stone-and-painted-stucco *chacmool*, or reclining male figure, at the entrance to the shrine of Tlaloc. It dates from one of the earliest phases of construction and was later covered over by larger and grander constructions. The figure holds a bowl to receive offerings to the god.

Around the Templo Mayor were the temple pyramids dedicated to Tezcatlipoca, Tonatiuh the sun god, Cihuacoatl, and a host of other deities. A special temple housed the foreign gods, whose cult images had been brought there after their people had been conquered. The Aztecs had an acquisitive religion, which reinforced their political goals; they were always ready to add new gods to the ones they already had, just as they were always ready to add new polities to the empire. Facing the Templo Mayor was the circular temple of Ehecatl (Wind), where the doorway was configured as a monstrous open mouth. Behind it, an I-shaped ball court hosted the Aztec version of the pan-Mesoamerican ritual ball game—a cross between soccer and basketball that was played with solid rubber balls.

Bordering the Templo Mayor to the north, archaeologists have excavated the Eagle House, the compound where the principal warriors met. There, the rooms were like atriums, open to the sky in the center and flanked by low benches where the warriors would gather to discuss strategies of conquest and the qualities of their enemies. Painted relief carvings along the face of the benches bear an eternal procession of warriors moving toward an altar adorned with scenes of bloodletting. These bench reliefs look so much like those in similar courtyard rooms at Tula that they must have been carved in conscious imitation; their purpose was to recall Toltec greatness and to link the Aztec fighting men with those ancient Toltec warriors. Flanking the doorways between rooms, life-size ceramic figures of eagle warriors and death lords (now moved to inside the Templo Mayor Museum) once stood guard.

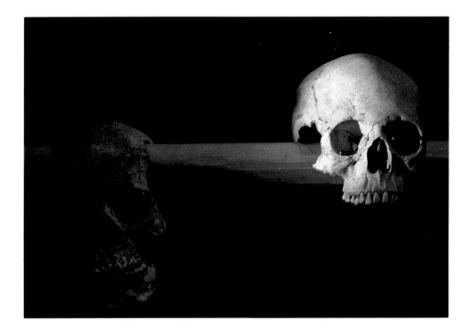

Smaller shrines and temples have been uncovered on either side of the Templo Mayor. A modest Red Temple imitates the architecture and painted imagery of ancient Teotihuacan. There are two shrines totally faced with carved stone skulls.

The 16th-century writers describe other shrines, features, and ritual platforms that have not yet been found archaeologically. Cortés wrote to his king that the precinct contained as many as 40 temple pyramids. As has already been mentioned, a large, round gladiatorial stone elevated on a low platform was the scene of ritual combat in honor of Xipe Totec. The conquerors and chroniclers were particularly astonished to see the main *tzompantli*, or skull rack, a wooden scaffold where the severed heads of sacrificial victims were strung side by side on crossbeams. The Spaniard Andrés de Tapia estimated that more than 136,000 skulls were hung there. No outline of the rack has been found on the ground, although excavators have found skulls with holes broken out on both sides, and part of Tlatelolco's skull rack has been excavated. Sahagún wrote in his history that there were several skull racks that received the skulls from different temples.

The ritual precinct of Tenochtitlan was a dazzling sight, with grand temples on top of lofty pyramids and great courtyards and avenues, all of which were plastered white and kept scrupulously clean. As Bernal Díaz remarked, "everything was whitened and polished, indeed the whole place was so clean that there was not a straw or a grain of dust to be found there." Aztec architects largely followed the building traditions of their Teotihuacan and Toltec predecessors, using coarse facing stones over rubble to define the mass of their pyramids, but relying on a plaster coat to make the final surface smooth and crisp. Now that the years have scoured away the plaster surface, all that remains is the rough sub-face. Stripped of its whiteness and edge, the architecture may appear crude to us, and, indeed, Aztec architecture was less elegant than it was functional and dramatic. The Aztecs did not channel their aesthetic energies as much into their buildings as they did into their stone sculpture.

THE STONES OF MEXICO

The glory and fame of the Aztecs live in their stone sculpture. Aztec carvers created one of the world's strongest sculptural traditions, with powerful conceptions that both impress and intimidate. Mastering a style that combined naturalism with abstraction, the sculptors achieved forms that were true to life but rendered with boldness and simplicity. They excelled at creating sculptures

The stone skull-rack altar to the north of the Templo Mayor is a reminder of the tzompantli. Inside the altar, archaeologists have found jaguar bones, musical instruments, and ceramic effigies of the gods. Archaeologists have yet to decipher the significance of the structure.

After priests ripped the heart from the chest of a living sacrificial victim, they flung the organ into a vessel like the cylindrical cavity set into the back of this massive, carved stone jaguar. The jaguar represented one of the highest military orders and was associated with Tezcatlipoca, patron of rulers. As such, it was a fitting recipient of sacrifices. This famous sculpture was found in 1900, not far from the site of the Templo Mayor.

of enormous size and weight. Even the smallest Aztec sculptures have a monumentality about them, but the large stones are astounding. Today, they remain some of the most powerful sculptures ever carved. Just as centuries ago the Aztec rulers lauded the achievements of their sculptors, these sculptures still call up praise in the 20th century. As sculptor Henry Moore once said: "Mexican sculpture seems to me to be true and right. Its 'stoniness,' by which I mean its truth to material, its tremendous power without loss of sensitiveness, its astonishing variety and fertility of form invention and its approach to a full three-dimensional conception of form, make it unsurpassed in my opinion by any other period of stone sculpture."

Relief carvings and three-dimensional stone images embellished the ritual precinct, palaces, and temples. Away from these centers, reliefs also appeared on boulders and on the face of cliffs in specially designated or sacred places. For example, Nezahualcoyotl adorned the solid rock of the hillside near his country palace at Tetzcotzingo with sculptures and carvings; and on the cliffs at Chapultepec, the Mexica rulers chose to have their portraits carved. The Aztecs filled their world with sculpture. Within the ritual precinct, carvings expressed the cosmic order: they commemorated secular events and recast them in a divine light, they held sacred blood, and they represented the gods.

The Stone of the Sun, better known as the Aztec Calendar Stone (*see page 92*), outlined the cosmos and expressed the apprehensions of the Fifth Age. It may have been laid flat on a platform before the sun temple, where its message would have been especially appropriate. Bordering the 10-foot-wide (3-meter-wide) circle are two great Fire Serpents, bearers of time, their long-snouted heads at the bottom and their pointed tails at the top; stylized flames issue from their body plates. They encircle the sun disk, characterized by eight pointed rays around a ring that contains the 20 day signs. In the center of the sun disk is the date 4 Movement, the date of the Fifth Sun. The dates of the previous suns are carved in the arms of the Movement glyph. In the very center is the frontal face not of the sun but of the earth, or night sun, flanked by monstrous claws holding hearts. All this imagery works together to convey the understanding that this fifth sun, which follows on the four previously destroyed suns, is precariously balanced. Without human hearts, it and time itself will be destroyed by the moving earth, whose fearsome visage appears in the center.

The victory stone of an Aztec ruler memorialized his triumphs and conquests, and was set up within the sacred precinct of Tenochtitlan. The carved panels surrounding the Stone of Moctezuma the Elder, shown at right, portray the ruler costumed as Huitzilopochtli defeating the gods of enemy cities. Over the top surface, the rayed disk of the sun received sacrificial blood in its central cavity.

Coatlicue, mother of Huitzilopochtli and earth mother of the Mexica, represented both life and death for the Aztecs. This terrifying statue of the serpent-skirted goddess, with snake's heads rearing from her decapitated body and a necklace of hands and hearts, was found in 1790. During the 1800s, nervous local authorities twice reburied the 8-foot-high (nearly 3-meter-high) stone monolith before finally placing it in a museum. The statue is now housed in the National Museum of Anthropology in Mexico City. This three-quarter back view shows how the statue appears to lean forward over the viewer.

Other sculptures also spoke of time and the cosmos. Smaller sun stones conveyed the message that the Fifth Sun followed on four previous ones. In front of the Templo Mayor, two "altars of skulls" were burying places for the stone replicas of year bundles, conceived as bundles of reeds. Although the year-bundle sculptures were not themselves visible after they were buried, the altars reminded people that the Aztecs had already bound and buried many 52-year cycles.

Here and there around the precinct were the victory monuments of the rulers. They expressed the position of Tenochtitlan as the center of the cosmos and doubled as gladiatorial and sacrificial stones, at the same time that they celebrated the victories of the rulers. Moctezuma the Elder's victory stone presents the sun on its upper surface and, all around the sides, shows the ruler in the guise of Huitzilopochtli capturing the deities of enemy altepeme. Panels showing elements of sacrifice—hearts, hands, skulls, symbols of preciosity—define Moctezuma's world as one of victory and expansion. One can picture the captives from these wars being sacrificed on top of the sun disk, their blood pooling in the circular cavity at the center of the sun, which their hearts will metaphorically nourish. Tizoc's monument was more elaborate than his valiant grandfather's, although Tizoc himself was an ineffective warrior. Despite his failure on the battlefield, he presented himself as Huitzilopochtli, capturing the deities of foreign polities and claiming victories that actually may have been those of his predecessors. A celestial band represents the sky above, and the pointed scales of the earth crocodile describe the earth below. Tizoc's victories occupy all the space in between. The sun disk carved on top has a depression in its center to receive the hearts that were offered there. Other rulers also had monuments carved to celebrate their victories in battle as well as their accomplishments at home.

These monuments were personal commemorations as well as loci for sacrifice. The Aztecs would probably have described them as eagle vessels, vessels to contain human hearts. Most eagle vessels were low, round basins. Some that have survived are 2 or 3 feet (about 1 meter) across and could have held a great quantity of precious liquid. Other examples are small and portable, delicately carved of greenstone; these generally feature the sun disk carved within the cavity, a rim of stylized human hearts, and outer walls carved as a row of eagle feathers. On the bottom appears the form of the earth lord, Tlaltecuhtli. One of the masterpieces of Aztec sculpture is the monumental eagle vessel carved as a crouching jaguar. Set into the feline's back is a cavity lined with eagle feathers. On the flat base, the sculptor carved the images of the gods Tezcatlipoca and Huitzilopochtli drawing blood from their own ears with bone awls. The message is clear: just as the gods gave their own blood, so should the Aztecs fill this huge eagle vessel with human blood.

Liberally placed around the ritual precinct were stone images of plants, animals, and "humans." The plants, such as cacti and squash, clearly pertained to agricultural abundance. The animals—including coyotes, rabbits, and toads—had their own different cult associations. They were depicted lifesize and in monumental form. Particularly numerous were the rattlesnakes, carved in just about every conceivable way—large and small, coiled and knotted, smooth or scaled, feathered, or laced with ears of corn. No creature appears more frequently in Aztec art than the rattlesnake. Its habit of shedding its skin and renewing itself link it with agricultural fertility, and, like the eagle and the jaguar, the serpent is a lethal carnivore.

Many of the anthropomorphic cult figures within the ritual precinct were made of wood or amaranth-seed dough. They did not survive. Nor did the cult figures encrusted with precious stones and metals, for those were particularly attractive targets for the conquerors. The figures that did survive were the durable stone sculptures, some appearing fully costumed and others carved nude so that they could be decorated with ritual attire during feasts.

An extraordinary class of these cult images were the macabre figures of the crouching Earth Lord (Tlaltecuhtli), the Cihuapipiltin (deified women who died in childbirth), and the Coatlicues. These figures share attributes that link them to the earth, death, and sacrifice. The Earth Lords, with fanged faces on their joints and wearing skirts decorated with skulls and crossed bones, were often carved in relief on the underside of monuments; although these reliefs were not then visible, they served to complete the monument, to ground it to the earth. The Cihuapipiltin were incarnate as fierce kneeling women, with skeletal faces and dangerous grasping claws. Most frightening of all were the Coatlicues, whose images were characterized by the dangerous aspects of the others but who additionally wore skirts of intertwined rattlesnakes.

The colossal effigy known simply as "the Coatlicue" is a profoundly disturbing, horrific image. We see it as such today, and the Aztecs, who understood the full meaning of its terrible imagery, must have felt so, too. In Moctezuma the Younger's time, there were more of these monumental sculptures—probably six—placed around the Templo Mayor. Today, only fragments of some of the others remain. The sculpture is the figure of a woman, more than 8 feet (nearly 3 meters) high, who wears a skirt of intertwined rattlesnakes (thus her name, Coatlicue, Serpents Her Skirt) and a serpent belt tied in front. Partially covering her hanging breasts is a necklace of alternating human hearts and hands, with a skull pendant in front. Her feet are the talons of a raptorial bird, such as an eagle, but animated with monstrous eyes. Her arms, bent at the elbows, rise up in front, but instead of hands, blood serpents flow out of her wrists; paper panels hang down in front. She is decapitated; two blood serpents rise from her neck, their heads meeting in the center to form the monstrous face that we read as the face of the deity. The figure looms forward in space, visually aggressive and menacing. From a distance, it appears like a cruciform block; up close, one's eye catches the violence of the imagery.

Flint knives inlaid with shell and obsidian were among the more than 7000 items—together with beads, shells, jade carvings, bones, and plant remains—placed within the Templo Mayor pyramid as offerings to Huitzilopochtli and Tlaloc.

How is one to understand a sculpture like this? More than simply a statue of Coatlicue, the mother of Huitzilopochtli, the figure is a study in human sacrifice. She wears the emblems of sacrifice (the hearts and the hands), but she herself has been mutilated; her own blood flows from these wounds. Her costume links her to the voracious Earth Lord, while her talons relate her to the eagle as sun. Very probably she is one of the Tzitzimime, the demons of death who will descend to devour humankind at the end of the Fifth Age. As such, she was every Aztec's nightmare.

THE IMPERIAL MESSAGE

The Templo Mayor was the ultimate proclamation of the imperial message. It was there that ritual sacrifice staved off the Tzitzimime and the chaos of destruction. It was there that the gods were nourished. It embodied Mexica power and domination. Tlaloc on the north and Huitzilopochtli on the south reflected the dual forces of agriculture and tribute that together fueled the empire. These forces were visibly expressed in the sculptural program, but they were also manifest in the more than 100 offertory caches that had been put into the pyramid of the Templo Mayor during its construction.

The archaeologists who dug into the pyramid discovered that many of the offerings had aquatic references. Many were items from the sea, such as coral, shells, sea urchins, sea snails, crocodile heads and skins, sawfish, other fish, turtles, and shark teeth. There were also many stone and ceramic images with marine associations: fish, turtles, and miniature boats carved out of stone, stone

Dogs filled both functional and symbolic roles in Aztec culture. They were kept for food, but also were often buried with the dead in the belief that their spirits could lead the deceased on the hazardous journey through the underworld.

Quetzalcoatl had many guises but is best known as the plumed serpent shown in this sculpture. Numerous sculptures of serpents, both plumed and not, have survived from Tenochtitlan. Most are also carved on the underside, with either the image of the Earth Lord or the serpent's own coils and scales.

Offerings to Tlaloc and Huitzilopochtli were often placed in cists, or small chambers. The cache shown here includes urns, stone face masks of Mezcala style, shells, precious stones, and bones. Offerings also were buried in lidded stone boxes, while many others were simply scattered loosely onto the soil, which was later covered during construction. Precious antiques and objects from the distant reaches of the empire signaled that imperial territory and history culminated at the Templo Mayor.

carvings of Tlaloc, ceramic effigy vessels of Tlaloc, and masks of Tlaloc. A dozen or so caches contained a seated image of the god of abundance. Thus the great pyramid was packed like a fruitcake with aquatic nuggets. Metaphorically, these nuggets of meaning transformed the pyramid into the Mountain of Sustenance, the mythical mountain filled with water that is the source of all agricultural abundance. From the altar of toads at the bottom to the chacmool altar at the top, the Tlaloc side of the Templo Mayor expressed the fundamental importance of agricultural fertility.

Offertory caches also reflected the empire's capacity to draw tribute from the most distant regions. Mezcala-style stone masks and figurines from Guerrero were included in the caches in great quantity. Small alabaster sculptures of sensitively carved deer heads and seated deities came from Puebla, rain-god sculptures came from Oaxaca, and crocodiles and jaguars came from the tropical rain forests of Veracruz, Tabasco, and Chiapas. Many of the aquatic items originated in the distant seas of the Pacific and the Gulf of Mexico. Mingled with these symbolic tribute items and with the emblems of agricultural abundance were signs of the past. A stunning Olmec stone mask, carved more than 2000 years before its burial, and two magnificently carved Teotihuacan masks, created around A.D. 600, were found among the cache offerings.

The chroniclers tell how Moctezuma The Younger invited the lords and peoples from throughout the empire to contribute precious stones and valuable items to be buried within the pyramid of the Templo Mayor, which the people did in great numbers. Items of value from the periphery came to the center, expressing in physical terms its predominant role. Precious and sacred items from the past linked the Mexica with ancient cultures. The long past and the broad expanse of the present came together in the cache offerings to proclaim the Templo Mayor as the focal point of time and space.

If the pyramid of the Templo Mayor was both the Mountain of Sustenance and the center of the cosmos, it was also the mountain of the war god. Throughout the pyramid, offerings spoke of war and sacrifice. Flint knives, stuck upright in balls of copal resin, were placed in the caches in great quantities; many were enlivened with the face of the Flint Knife God, bearing teeth and eyes of shell, eyebrows of mosaic, and sometimes a little paint. There were also huge obsidian blades and many skulls, a large number of which were animated with round shell eyes and flint blades in their nose and mouth cavities. It was a pyramid shot through with the evidence of human blood shed in sacrifice.

Externally, the sculptural program transformed it into the mountain of Coatepec, the scene of Huitzilopochtli's miraculous birth and the defeat of his enemy sister, Coyolxauhqui. Serpent balustrades led up to the top, a massive undulating serpent wall flanked the base of the pyramid, and serpent heads jutted out from the walls of the pyramid all along Huitzilopochtli's side, making this pyramid into a serpent mountain, a Coatepec. At the foot of the stairs leading up to Huitzilopochtli's temple was the great relief carving of Coyolxauhqui. There she lay, stripped, decapitated, dismembered, her hair ornamented with the feather tufts of down that are symbolic of sacrifice. At the top of the long stairway, the cult image of Huitzilopochtli sat victorious. Huitzilopochtli's defeat over his sister and his 400 brothers became a metaphor for the Mexica's defeat of their enemies. Each sacrifice at the Templo Mayor was a reenactment of the god's victory. Just as Huitzilopochtli slew his sister and tossed her down the mountain of Coatepec, the captives offered in sacrifice to him were slain and rolled down the stairs, reinforcing over and over again the idea that the Aztecs ruled because of the victory of their patron deity.

Each sacrifice and each ritual at the Templo Mayor, on the Tlaloc as well as the Huitzilopochtli side, activated the messages of imperial domination embodied in the Templo Mayor. The pyramid was both Mountain of Sustenance and Mountain of the Serpent; it was fertile earth and victorious warrior-sun. Processions came and went from this center back and forth from the periphery. Ceremonial activities extended the sacred power of the precinct throughout the city and valley beyond, linking the urban temples with shrines on the surrounding mountain tops and binding the valley together in chains of energy. Lords from allied and provincial altepeme came to see and participate in these ceremonies, learning anew that the message of the Templo Mayor was the validity of Mexica rule.

The nighttime glow of Mexico City bathes the Plaza of the Three Cultures, where a colonial-era church and monastery overlook the remains of
here, in 1521, that the remnants of the Aztec empire under Cuauhtemoc surrendered to the Spaniards. In 1960, archaeologists began excavating

the main temple pyramid of Tlatelolco. It was
the ruins of the temple pyramid.

9

THE FALL
OF THE EMPIRE

From where the eagles are resting,
from where the jaguars are exalted,
the Sun is invoked.
Like a shield that descends,
so does the Sun set.
In Mexico night is falling,
war rages on all sides.
Oh Giver of Life!
war comes near.

Proud of itself
is the City of Mexico-Tenochtitlan.
Here no one fears to die in war.
This is our glory.
This is Your Command,
oh Giver of Life!
Have this in mind, oh princes,
do not forget it.
Who could conquer Tenochtitlan?
Who could shake the foundation of heaven?

The Aztec poet who wrote this Nahuatl poem pro-
claiming the glory of the people of the sun, the
eagles, and the jaguars knows with all his heart that the
people of Mexico-Tenochtitlan are invincible. Yet war
burns all around, and seeds of doubt take root. Like the
poet, we wonder how this strong and fearsome empire, the
master of Mesoamerica, could have been conquered and
destroyed by a small band of Spanish adventurers. How
could the empire collapse so suddenly and completely?

Moctezuma II, the ruler of the Mexica at the time of the arrival of Cortés, was the great-grandson of Moctezuma I and the earthly representative of Huitzilopochtli. Shown below is Moctezuma's image and name-glyph from the *Codex Mendoza*.

The answer lies in the nature of the empire, in the relations between the Triple Alliance center and the provinces. Cortés' arrival touched off what was essentially an indigenous revolution against the Mexica-dominated empire. From the very beginning, when the Spaniards first visited Cempoala, on the Gulf Coast, Cortés learned that the Aztec empire was a network of independent-thinking *altepeme* (towns), many of which chafed under the Aztec yoke. Throughout his campaign, he sought to drive a wedge between the Mexica Aztecs and the other peoples allied with them. He learned that strong peoples like the Tlaxcalans and Huejotzinga, among others, had never been brought under imperial rule and were avowed enemies of the Aztecs. Cortés consciously fanned the fires of Tlaxcalan enmity, convincing them to strike out against their old oppressors. In the end, most of the altepeme in and around the Valley of Mexico joined the fight against the Mexica. When the final siege of Tenochtitlan reached its climax, 900 Spaniards and more than 150,000 native allies invaded the island city. The Spaniards, who wrote most of the accounts of the campaign, saw it as the Spanish conquest of Mexico, and this is the story that has endured. But the allied altepeme saw it as an indigenous revolution that would free them from Mexica domination. It was only later that they realized they, too, had been conquered.

From the beginning, Moctezuma the Younger thought the Spaniards might be supernaturals. Never before had the Aztecs seen horses, guns and cannon, steel and iron. The bulky Spanish ships, like floating towers, were strange. The men who arrived in them, clothed and armed in steel, were even stranger, with white "chalky faces," yellow hair, and long, yellow beards. Moctezuma suspected that Cortés might be the returning Topiltzin Quetzalcoatl (Our Prince, Feathered Serpent), the Toltec ruler and culture hero who, according to the old legends, had sailed off to the east on a raft of serpents in the year 1 Reed, vowing to return one day to reclaim his throne. For 10 years, a series of omens in Mexico forewarned calamity. Then, in 1 Reed (1519), Cortés landed on the Gulf Coast. Moctezuma feared in his heart that Topiltzin Quetzalcoatl had returned. He spoke of Cortés as a *teotl* (deity), and immediately sent him the costumes of Quetzalcoatl, Tezcatlipoca, and Tlaloc. On the shore of the eastern sea, the emperor's ambassadors greeted Cortés, dressed him in the array of Quetzalcoatl, and explained how Moctezuma had been watching over Mexico for him. Much later, after the Spaniards had been in Mexico several months and some of their number had been killed in battle, Moctezuma must have suspected that they were not returning gods after all, but he could never be absolutely sure. The prophesies had been strong, and the Spaniards acted like no humans he had known before. And they had machines that could blow up a mountain or pulverize trees (the cannons), and deer as tall as rooftops to carry them around (the horses). Moctezuma, a pious man who knew that one lived according to the destinies carried by the *tonalpohualli* (day-count), could not afford to offend the supernaturals, if indeed they be.

Cortés set out from the Gulf Coast with 400 Spaniards, 16 horses, and several cannon. Almost immediately, and then all along his route, he increased his forces by pitting Aztec vassal states against the imperial center. The Tlaxcalans agreed to join Cortés because they shared his goal of subduing the Mexica. The map shows the route taken by Cortés' forces in the advance to Tenochtitlan, as well as the retreat of the invaders in the aftermath of Noche Triste (sorrowful night).

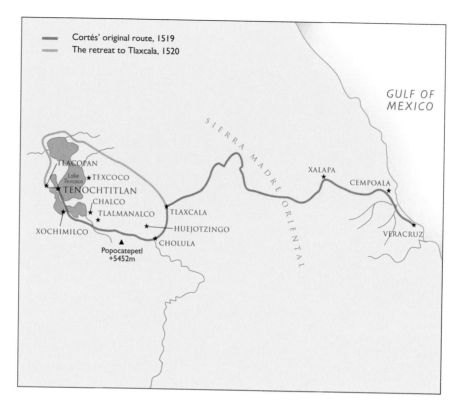

Cortés, for his part, successfully played the Mexica against their enemies throughout his campaign. For example, he convinced the Cempoallans, who had just come under Aztec domination, to imprison the imperial tax collectors; this brave act effectively forced the Cempoallans to side with the Spaniards against Moctezuma, and it gained Cortés a reputation for boldness. Then he secretly released the tax collectors and sent them home with a message of friendship for their emperor. He thereby allied himself with both the Cempoallans and the Mexica while pitting them against each other. Throughout the campaign, Cortés' allies would provide him with the supply lines he sorely needed in enemy territory.

With Cempoallan forces accompanying him, Cortés marched into Tlaxcala. Bloody battles ensued, claiming lives on both sides, but the outnumbered Spaniards prevailed. Their steel weapons easily cut through the indigenous wood and leather shields, their horses gave them mobility, and their guns terrified as they killed. The Spaniards and Tlaxcalans fought different battles with different aims. While the Spaniards launched coordinated attacks of various kinds to divide and vanquish their adversaries, the Tlaxcalans followed the native custom of a more highly ritualized warfare. They advanced in a closed body, which meant that only a small portion of their fighting force engaged the enemy at a time. Then the bravest captains, easily identifiable by their flamboyant and cumbersome costumes, took great risks in hand-to-hand combat in order to capture prisoners. When an indigenous ruler or a number of the principal captains were slain, the other warriors stopped fighting and withdrew. The Tlaxcalans, like the Aztecs, sought not victory on the battlefield but prisoners for the sacrificial stone. Spanish weapons and different fighting goals gave the invaders the edge throughout the Mexican conflict.

Once it became clear that the Tlaxcalans could not easily defeat the Spaniards, the Tlaxcalans agreed to peace. They listened to Cortés' desire to subdue the Mexica, and, sharing his goals, they agreed to combine forces with him. The neighboring Huejotzinga joined also.

To the Mexica, Cortés still presented a neutral front. Moctezuma sent ambassadors to woo Cortés away from a Tlaxcalan alliance, which the emperor knew would be dangerous. Cortés amiably reassured the ambassadors that he wished only to visit and pay his respects to the emperor. Moctezuma's emissaries stayed with Cortés to keep an eye on him and, ostensibly, to guide him into Tenochtitlan.

They journeyed by way of Cholula, a great pilgrimage center that was allied with the Mexica and the enemy of the Tlaxcalans. There, the

On their westward march, Cortés and his Cempoallan allies had to cross the Sierra Madre Oriental, a daunting range of mountains and deep valleys separating the Gulf Coast from the high interior. The winding trails that run along the ridge tops may have encouraged the Aztecs to think of their roads as serpents.

Cholula had been a major pilgrimage center for more than a thousand years before the Spanish arrived. In Aztec times, it thrived as a cult center for Quetzalcoatl. Cholula's great pyramid was the largest in Mesoamerica, and was so massive that the Spaniards built an entire monastery on its summit. Today, in the shadow of the majestic volcano Popacatepetl (Smoking Mountain), the ruined pyramid resembles a steep hill rising from the surrounding plain. During the Spanish invasion, Cortés feared an ambush at Cholula; with the aid of his Tlaxcalan allies he struck first, massacring thousands of Cholulans in their main plaza.

Tlaxcalans convinced the Spanish that a fatal ambush awaited them. The Spaniards, Tlaxcalans, and Cempoallans attacked first, however. They called the Cholulans into the vast courtyard of their main temple, sealed the entrances, and proceeded to massacre 4000 to 5000 citizens; then they looted the city. It is hard to say whether this action was intended merely to prevent an ambush, but it had the additional effects of rewarding the Tlaxcalans for their allegiance and disheartening the Aztecs.

Moctezuma became increasingly distraught at the news that reached him about the Spaniards and their growing army. He wished to stop their advance into Tenochtitlan, but at the same time he wanted to avoid direct confrontation. He even forbade his imperial allies from attacking the Spaniards. Instead, the emperor sent sorcerers to cast spells on them and emissaries with gifts to dissuade the conqueror from continuing, and he also set up roadblocks. None of these strategies worked, however, for Cortés would not be detoured. He continued toward Mexico-Tenochtitlan. The Aztecs later recalled the sight of the Spanish forces: "[The Spaniards] came grouped, they came assembled, they came raising dust. Their iron lances [and] the halberds seemed to glisten, and their iron swords were wavy, like a water [course]. Their cuirasses [and] their helmets seemed to resound. And some came all in iron; they came turned into iron; they came gleaming. Hence they went causing great astonishment; hence they went causing great fear."

Meanwhile, in Tenochtitlan, an apprehensive quiet had settled on the city. The streets were left empty, and the people seemed resigned to whatever their fate might be. Sahagún's noble informants recalled how the people of the capital lamented: "Let it be thus. Let it be accursed. For already we are to die, already we are to perish. Yea, already we await our death."

Finally, Cortés advanced on the southern causeway that led into Tenochtitlan. Moctezuma sent his relatives, rulers of other imperial cities, to greet him. Crowds of people from all over gathered to see the Spaniards. Then the emperor himself came forth to welcome Cortés into his city. Still fearing that the newcomers were returning gods, he proclaimed to Cortés: "O our lord. Thou hast come to arrive on earth. Thou hast come to govern the city of Mexico; thou hast come to descend upon thy mat, upon thy seat, which for a moment I have watched for thee, which I have guarded for thee. For thy governors are departed—the rulers Itzcoatl, Moctezuma the Elder, Axayacatl, Tizoc, Ahuitzotl, who yet a very short time ago had come to stand guard for thee, who had come to govern the city of Mexico.... The rulers departed maintaining that thou wouldst come to visit thy city, that thou wouldst come to descend upon thy mat, thy seat. And now it hath been fulfilled; thou hast come; thou has endured fatigue, thou hast endured weariness. Peace be with thee. Rest thyself. Visit thy palace."

Moctezuma led the Spaniards to fine accommodations in his father Axayacatl's palace. Some days later, he gave Cortés and his captains a tour of his great city, showing off the vast marketplace, the tall temple pyramids, and the splendor of Tenochtitlan. The Spaniards, seeing the perilous position they were in—essentially trapped in a potentially hostile country—realized that their continued existence depended on the person of Moctezuma.

In an extraordinary move, Cortés took the emperor hostage. Moctezuma's court—those who could—fled; his Mexica followers soon turned away from him, and he was left isolated from his people. His lords and allies were disgusted that he had allowed the Spaniards into the very heart of the city, where they were already beginning to plunder the treasuries and raid the temples, smashing the cult images. Moctezuma's nephew Cacama, the ruler of Texcoco, plotted to overthrow his uncle, but he himself was tricked and became another of Cortés' captives.

The increasing tension came to a disastrous climax while Cortés was temporarily out of the city. On short notice, Cortés had taken most of his men east to the Gulf Coast in order to intercept a group of Spaniards sent by the Cuban governor to arrest him for disobeying orders. While Cortés defused this threat, Pedro de Alvarado was left in charge in Tenochtitlan. It was the time of a major festival in honor of Huitzilopochtli; the careful preparations had all been made, and the warriors gathered in Huitzilopochtli's courtyard to dance the celebration. At this point, Alvarado and his men surrounded the courtyard and began to slaughter the unarmed

PREVIOUS PAGE: **The first encounter between Cortés and Moctezuma took place on the southern causeway leading into Tenochtitlan. This reconstruction shows Cortés advancing to meet the supreme Aztec ruler. Walking just behind the Spaniard is Malinche, also known as Doña Marina, a Tabascan woman who acted as his translator and subsequently became his companion.**

celebrants. Astonished and outraged at this action, the Mexica quickly gathered their arms and attacked the Spaniards ferociously, driving them back to Axayacatl's palace.

When Cortés arrived back in Tenochtitlan with reinforcements, the city was temporarily quiet, but any chance of a peaceful alliance had been lost. Fighting soon began again in earnest. Moctezuma was killed in the ensuing chaos, and his brother Cuitlahuac, who had always urged resistance to the Spanish, became *Huey Tlatoani* (Great Speaker). He continued to attack the Spaniards relentlessly. Seeing that they were trapped and losing men rapidly, the Spaniards determined to flee the city, taking with them what noble hostages they still had. On a drizzly night in June 1520, they fought their way out and over the shortest causeway to the mainland on the west, harassed and attacked on all sides by the Mexica. All the hostages, 600 to 700 Spaniards, and 2000 to 3000 Tlaxcalans died in the terrible fighting; their bodies filled the canals. Just over 400 Spaniards survived the exodus, and all were wounded. Later, the Spaniards called that night Noche Triste, sorrowful night.

From this ignominious defeat, Cortés, his men, and the Tlaxcalan allies limped back to Tlaxcala, harried by Mexica armies for most of the way. In Tlaxcala, they recuperated for five-and-a-half months, building strength for a renewed campaign. Reinforcements and arms arrived from Cuba to bolster Spanish resolve. Cortés determined to isolate Mexico-Tenochtitlan from the countryside and weaken it with a siege before entering it again.

Meanwhile, in Tenochtitlan, an epidemic of smallpox had broken out. This Old World disease had arrived with the Spaniards, and had spread quickly through the indigenous population, which had no resistance to it. Cuitlahuac died of the disease after ruling Mexico only 80 days. His cousin Cuauhtemoc (Descending Eagle) succeeded him. Later the Aztecs recalled the devastation: "There came to be prevalent a great sickness, a plague.... Some it indeed covered [with pustules];.... Many indeed died of it. No longer could they walk; they only lay in their abodes, in their beds. No longer could they move,...no longer could they raise themselves.... There was much perishing. Like a covering...were the pustules. Indeed, many people died of them, and many just died of hunger. There was death from hunger; there was no one to take care of another; there was no one to attend to another." As many as half the people in the city may have died in the epidemic.

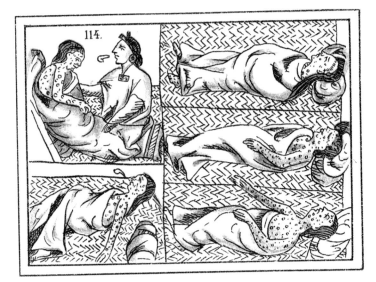

The Spaniards unwittingly brought with them a weapon of great power: smallpox. The indigenous population had virtually no immunity to this and other European diseases. This image from the *Florentine Codex* records the spread of the disease: as many as half the people of Mexico-Tenochtitlan are thought to have died in the epidemic of 1520, including Cuitlahuac, successor to Moctezuma.

In May 1521, Cortés and his indigenous allies commenced the final assault on Tenochtitlan. Despite fierce opposition from the Mexica warriors, the invaders prevailed: the once majestic city fell and was completely destroyed in the fighting. The siege lasted nearly three months. This page from the *Codex Moctezuma* shows the desperate fighting that took place for control of the Templo Mayor.

Cortés then laid siege to Tenochtitlan for three months, fighting nearly every day. The Spaniards had built boats to halt water traffic of food and supplies, and they blocked all the causeways. Texcoco, perhaps Tenochtitlan's oldest ally, had sided with the Spaniards following the death of its ruler Cacama, who perished as a Spanish hostage on the Noche Triste. Chalco, Tlalmanalco, Xochimilco, and most of the other lakeside cities followed Texcoco's lead. The Mexica stood almost alone against the combined forces of the Spaniards, their ancient Tlaxcalan enemies, and their former allies. The odds were overwhelmingly against them. Still, when the Mexica fought, their goal was the ancient one of taking sacrificial captives. The Mexica accounts of the conflict nearly always mention the captives taken, but never the enemies slain.

Native warriors were always prepared to end their earthly days on the sacrificial stone, where they would be transformed into companions of the sun, but the Spaniards thought this an inconceivably hideous death. Often the Spanish heard the devilish sound of drums, trumpets, and flutes and looked across to see their comrades upon the altar of Huitzilopochtli. Occasionally, they knew the captured horses were being sacrificed, too, their heads strung along with the human heads on the skull racks. In his old age, Bernal Díaz admitted that it was the fear of just such a death that caused "a sort of horror and gloom [to] seize in [his] heart" before each battle.

Ultimately, however, the horror of the Conquest was felt by the besieged and embattled Mexica. Those who were not killed in battle sickened and starved. As the Mexica later recalled: "There was hunger. Many died of famine. There was not more good, pure water to drink—only nitrous water. Many died of it—contracted dysentery, which killed them. The people ate anything—lizards, barn swallows, corn leaves, salt-grass; they gnawed...leather and buckskin, cooked or toasted; or [bitter] sedum and adobe bricks. Never had such suffering been seen; it was terrifying how many of us died when we were shut in as we were." Bernal Díaz remarked that, despite their hunger, the Mexica still did not eat the flesh of their own people, only that of enemy warriors captured in battle.

When they finally entered Tenochtitlan, the conquerors were astonished to discover the number of people who had perished in the city. The houses were full of corpses, and the streets so covered with piles of dead that the Mexica and conquerors alike were forced to walk on their bodies. Cortés wrote to his king, "indeed, so great was their suffering that it was beyond our understanding how they could endure it."

The Conquest razed the once-majestic city. Spaniards and allies consolidated the territory they took each day by pulling down all the buildings and filling the canals and breaks in the causeways with the rubble. They set fire to the houses so that no Mexica could take refuge there. The defending Mexica, in their turn, erected barricades and destroyed bridges even as they retreated deeper into the interior of the city. Incrementally and irreversibly, the proud city of Tenochtitlan disintegrated. By the time the Spaniards defeated the last pocket of resistance and, on August 13th, 1521, captured Cuauhtemoc, the Aztec capital was a wasteland. An elegy for Tenochtitlan reveals how totally the conquest crushed the Mexica:

> Broken spears lie in the roads;
> we have torn our hair in our grief.
> The houses are roofless now, and their walls
> are red with blood.
> Worms are swarming in the streets and plazas,
> and the walls are splattered with gore.
> The water has turned red, as if it were dyed,
> and when we drink it,
> it has the taste of brine.
> We have pounded our hands in despair
> against the adobe walls,
> for our inheritance, our city, is lost and dead.
> The shields of our warriors were its defense,
> but they could not save it.

Just two years earlier, when Cortés first walked along the southern causeway into Mexico-Tenochtitlan in 1519, the capital of the Aztec empire shone resplendent in the lake. His men were so astonished that they thought they must be dreaming. Tenochtitlan was the largest and most well-ordered place anyone had ever seen, with broad, clean avenues, a sparkling network of canals, and stuccoed temple pyramids that rose above the houses and palaces. The capital would enter the encyclopedias and compendia of Europe as one of the majestic island cities of the world. On the day of Cortés' arrival, crowds of prosperous citizens milled around him and his men; the lake was filled with canoes. The inhabitants had come on foot and across the water to see the curious strangers, about whom they had heard such exaggerated rumors. Moctezuma and his court came out in unparalleled finery to greet him. Cortés embraced the most powerful human in Mexico, one who inspired awe everywhere around him. Within two years, all this had been brought down. Moctezuma and his successor were both dead, the city destroyed. The Triple Alliance had splintered.

What had held the Aztec empire together and what had supported the opulence of Tenochtitlan was a set of alliances between individual peoples. Some had been won by force and intimidation, others had come voluntarily, but never were they permanently tied. The empire was always a collection of independent-minded altepeme, each with its own identity. After years of Mexica

The *Lienzo de Tlaxcala*, a post-Conquest pictorial chronicle, depicts the final stages of the destruction of Tenochtitlan. In this scene, the captive Cuauhtemoc surrenders before Cortés. In the custom befitting an Aztec warrior, Cuauhtemoc begged the victors to put him to death. Instead, Cortés spared him—in Aztec eyes, a far worse fate. Four years later, however, the Spaniards ingloriously murdered Cuauhtemoc.

ycpolinhq mexica

domination, they severed their ties when the opportunity arose, looking for autonomy, which Cortés naturally promised. The loose structure of the empire was the weapon of its own destruction.

The Mexica's understanding of the world and their place within it had worked against them throughout the campaign. Moctezuma felt powerless to prevent the ancient prophecies from being fulfilled, for he and his people were governed by the reading of the omens and the day-count. In any case, he could not conceivably go into battle without first negotiating the terms and embracing the act with all the correct gestures and rituals, for battles were waged on behalf of the gods. Only after his young warriors had been slaughtered while dancing in the festival to Huitzilopochtli did his forces set aside ancient customs and attack the Spaniards furiously. By then it was too late; the Spaniards had gained too many allies, and the indigenous revolution had been set in motion.

The identities of the peoples who came under Triple Alliance control had always rested with their altepetl, not with the empire. When the Spaniards helped to cut the cords that tied them together, the altepeme sprang back to self-government. They dealt with the Spaniards not as Aztecs but as Tlaxcalans, Texcoca, Xochimilca, and Chalca. In the years following the conquest of Mexico-Tenochtitlan, as wave after wave of disease decimated them and as the Spanish administrative system spread across the land, the people of the altepeme continued to fight in the Spanish courts for the rights and privileges they had earned helping to overthrow the Culhua-Mexica.

REFERENCES

CHAPTER 1: A SPLENDID WORLD APART
The original chroniclers continue to be among the best guides to the Aztec world. Their writings speak so eloquently about what they saw and understood, and they embody the flavor of the period and the culture. Throughout this book, I have returned to the original sources as much as possible. The two most important eyewitness accounts by Spanish conquerors are the five letters Hernán Cortés wrote to Charles V during the Conquest, and the history of the Conquest written by Bernal Díaz del Castillo. The Spanish friars Diego Durán, Motolinía, and Bernardino de Sahagún all relied upon native informants and native texts for their important accounts of Aztec life. The indigenous perspective is also represented by histories written by the sons of Aztec royalty, such as Hernando Alvarado Tezozomoc and Fernando de Alva Ixtlilxochitl. Of the modern overviews of Aztec culture, those by Frances Berdan and Jacques Soustelle are among the most comprehensive. I especially relied on Berdan's detailed study and recommend it highly.

ALVA IXTLILXOCHITL, FERNANDO DE 1975 *Obras históricas*, edited by Edmundo O'Gorman. 2 vols. Universidad Nacional Autónoma de México, Mexico.

ALVARADO TEZOZOMOC, HERNANDO 1975 *Cronica Mexicana*, edited by Manuel Orozco y Berra. Editorial Porruá, Mexico.

BERDAN, FRANCES F. 1982 *The Aztecs of Central Mexico: An Imperial Society.* Case Studies in Cultural Anthropology. Holt, Rinehart and Winston, New York.

CORTÉS, HERNÁN 1986 *Hernán Cortés: Letters from Mexico*, edited and translated by Anthony Pagden. Yale University Press, New Haven.

DÍAZ DEL CASTILLO, BERNAL 1983 *The Conquest of New Spain*, edited and translated by J. M. Cohen. Penguin Books, New York.

DURÁN, DIEGO 1964 *The Aztecs: The History of the Indies of New Spain*, edited and translated by Doris Heyden and Fernando Horcasitas. Orion Press, New York.

1971 *The Book of the Gods and Rites and the Ancient Calendar* edited and translated by Fernando Horcasitas and Doris Heyden. University of Oklahoma Press, Norman.

MOTOLINÍA 1951 *Motolinía's History of the Indians of New Spain*, edited and translated by Frances Borgia Steck. Academy of American Franciscan History, Washington, D.C.

SAHAGÚN, BERNARDINO DE 1953-82 *Florentine Codex, General History of the Things of New Spain* (12 books), edited and translated by Arthur J. O. Anderson and Charles E. Dibble. School of American Research and the University of Utah, Santa Fe and Salt Lake City.

SOUSTELLE, JACQUES 1962 *The Daily Life of the Aztecs on the Eve of the Spanish Conquest.* The Macmillan Company, New York.

CHAPTER 2: ORIGINS
The best primary sources for the Aztec migration are Durán, Sahagún, and Alvarado Tezozomoc (whose account is similar to that recorded by Durán). In addition, Michael Smith has studied the reality of the migration accounts, and I have analyzed the migrations as cultural statements. For the archaeology of the Valley of Mexico, I recommend Muriel Porter Weaver's overview of Mesoamerican archaeology. For Teotihuacan and Tula, I recommend the volumes of articles edited by Janet Berlo and by Kathleen Berrin and Esther Pasztory as well as the monograph by Richard Diehl; the volume by William Sanders, Jeffrey Parsons, and Robert Santley takes an ecological approach to the cultures of the Valley of Mexico.

BERLO, JANET (EDITOR) 1992 *Art, Ideology, and the City of Teotihuacan.* Dumbarton Oaks, Washington, D.C.

BERRIN, KATHLEEN, AND ESTHER PASZTORY (EDITORS) 1993 *Teotihuacan: Art from the City of the Gods.* Thames and Hudson, New York.

BOONE, ELIZABETH HILL 1991 Migration Histories as Ritual Performance. In *To Change Place: Aztec Ceremonial Landscapes*, edited by Davíd Carrasco, pp.121-151. University Press of Colorado, Niwot.

DIEHL, RICHARD A. 1983 *Tula: The Toltec Capital of Ancient Mexico.* Thames and Hudson, New York.

SMITH, MICHAEL E. 1984 The Aztlan Migrations of the Nahuatl Chronicles: Myth or History? *Ethnohistory* 31(3): 153-186.

For the archaeology of the Valley of Mexico, see:

SANDERS, WILLIAM T., JEFFREY R. PARSONS, AND ROBERT S. SANTLEY 1979 *The Basin of Mexico: Ecological Processes in the Evolution of a Civilization.* Academic Press, New York.

WEAVER, MURIEL PORTER 1993 *The Aztecs, Maya, and Their Predecessors: Archaeology of Mesoamerica.* Third edition. Academic Press, San Diego.

CHAPTER 3: THE IMPERIAL STORY

The rich detail of the imperial story was recorded by Father Durán. I have relied extensively on his account. Among the modern histories, Nigel Davies' book is a detailed political/military history. Two historical novels by Frances Gillmor recapture the vibrancy of the early empire; I recommend them as highly enjoyable and informative.

DAVIES, NIGEL 1980 *The Aztecs.* University of Oklahoma Press, Norman.

GILLMOR, FRANCES 1977 *The King Danced in the Marketplace.* The University of Utah Press, Salt Lake City. (a biography of Moctezuma the Elder)

1983 *Flute of the Smoking Mirror: A Portrait of Nezahualcoyotl—Poet-King of the Aztecs.* The University of Utah Press, Salt Lake City.

CHAPTER 4: THE EMPIRE'S PEOPLE

Even more than Sahagún, the Spanish judge Alonso de Zorita is the major source for information on Aztec social structure and economics. James Lockhart gives an excellent explanation of the altepetl in his study of early colonial Aztecs. For the network of elites, see Michael Smith's article, and for more information on the Aztec household, see Susan Evans' article.

EVANS, SUSAN T. 1993 Aztec Household Organization and Village Administration. In *Prehispanic Domestic Units in Western Mesoamerica,* edited by Robert S. Santley and Kenneth G. Hirth, pp. 173-189. CRC Press, Boca Raton, Florida.

LOCKHART, JAMES 1992 *The Nahuas After the Conquest: A Social and Cultural History of the Indians of Central Mexico, Sixteenth Through Eighteenth Centuries.* Stanford University Press, Stanford, California.

SMITH, MICHAEL E. 1986 The Role of Social Stratification in the Aztec Empire: A View from the Provinces. *American Anthropologist* 88 (1): 70-91.

ZORITA, ALONSO DE 1963 *Life and Labor in Ancient Mexico: The Brief and Summary Relation of the Lords of New Spain,* edited and translated by Benjamin Keen. Rutgers University Press, New Brunswick, New Jersey.

CHAPTER 5: LIVING WELL AND PROSPERING

Much basic information on the Aztec economy is included in Father Sahagún's writings, especially the parts or "books" on the merchants, the people, and earthly things. The articles by Elizabeth Brumfiel and Mary Hodge, and the book by Ross Hassig, treat different aspects of the market economy. For the tribute economy, see especially the new edition of the *Codex Mendoza* by Frances Berdan and Patricia Anawalt.

BERDAN, FRANCES F., AND PATRICIA RIEFF ANAWALT (EDITORS) 1992 *The Codex Mendoza.* 4 volumes. University of California Press, Berkeley.

BRUMFIEL, ELIZABETH M. 1987 Elite and Utilitarian Crafts in the Aztec State. In *Specialization, Exchange, and Complex Societies,* edited by Elizabeth M. Brumfiel and Timothy K. Earle, pp. 102-118. Cambridge University Press, Cambridge.

CALNEK, EDWARD E. 1972 Settlement Pattern and Chinampa Agriculture at Tenochtitlan. *American Antiquity* 37 (1): 104-115.

HASSIG, ROSS 1985 *Trade, Tribute, and Transportation: The Sixteenth-Century Political Economy of the Valley of Mexico.* University of Oklahoma Press, Norman.

HODGE, MARY G. 1992 Aztec Market Systems. *National Geographic Research and Exploration* 8 (4): 428-445.

CHAPTER 6: THE COSMIC ORDER

The Spanish friars Diego Durán, Motolinía, and Bernardino de Sahagún all wrote firsthand descriptions of Aztec ideology. Alfonso Caso's *The Aztecs: People of the Sun* is a classic overview of Aztec religious beliefs. More detailed is H. B. Nicholson's review of the features of Aztec religion, which parallels Caso's article on the Aztec calendar; both are fundamental resources. My monograph looks into the conception and representation of deities.

BOONE, ELIZABETH HILL 1989 Incarnations of the Aztec Supernatural: The Image of Huitzilopochtli in Mexico and Europe. *Transactions of the American Philosophical Society,* vol. 79, part 2. Philadelphia.

CASO, ALFONSO 1958 *The Aztecs: People of the Sun.* University of Oklahoma Press, Norman.

1971 Calendrical Systems of Central Mexico. In *Handbook of Middle American Indians,* vol. 10, edited by Gordon F. Ekholm and Ignacio Bernal, pp. 333-348. Robert Wauchope, gen. ed. University of Texas Press, Austin.

NICHOLSON, H. B. 1971 Religion in Pre-Hispanic Central Mexico. In *Handbook of Middle American Indians,* vol. 10, edited by Gordon F. Ekholm and Ignacio Bernal, pp. 395-446. Robert Wauchope, gen. ed. University of Texas Press, Austin.

CHAPTER 7: A WORLD IN BALANCE

Miguel León-Portilla's books tap Sahagún and other Nahuatl sources to provide superb overviews of Aztec thought and literature. Louise Burkhart's study of postconquest Aztec morality also can help us understand preconquest moral constructs. Cecelia Klein gives a fine detailed discussion of Aztec bloodletting, and Inga Clendinnen offers insights about the place of human sacrifice in Aztec culture.

BURKHART, LOUISE M. 1989 *The Slippery Earth: Nahua-Christian Moral Dialogue in Sixteenth-Century Mexico.* University of Arizona Press, Tucson.

CLENDINNEN, INGA 1991 *Aztecs: An Interpretation.* Cambridge University Press, Cambridge.

KLEIN, CECELIA 1987 The Ideology of Autosacrifice at the Templo Mayor. In *The Aztec Templo Mayor.* edited by Elizabeth H. Boone, pp. 293-370. Dumbarton Oaks, Washington, D.C..

LEÓN-PORTILLA, MIGUEL 1963 *Aztec Thought and Culture.* University of Oklahoma Press, Norman.

1986 *Pre-Columbian Literatures of Mexico.* University of Oklahoma Press, Norman.

CHAPTER 8: THE HEART OF THE EMPIRE

The best books in English on Aztec sculpture are those by Richard Townsend, Esther Pasztory, and H. B. Nicholson. More recently, a number of publications have focused on the Templo Mayor and the rituals that energized it, offering some interesting perspectives. These include books by Eduardo Matos Moctezuma, Johanna Broda, and Davíd Carrasco, as well as volumes of articles edited by Carrasco and myself.

BOONE, ELIZABETH HILL (EDITOR) 1987 *The Aztec Templo Mayor.* Dumbarton Oaks, Washington, D.C.

BRODA, JOHANNA, DAVÍD CARRASCO, AND EDUARDO MATOS MOCTEZUMA 1987 *The Great Temple of Tenochtitlan: Center and Periphery in the Aztec World.* University of California Press, Berkeley.

CARRASCO, DAVÍD (EDITOR) 1991 *To Change Place: Aztec Ceremonial Landscapes.* University Press of Colorado, Niwot.

CARRASCO, DAVÍD, AND EDUARDO MATOS MOCTEZUMA 1992 *Moctezuma's Mexico: Visions of the Aztec World.* University Press of Colorado, Niwot.

MATOS MOCTEZUMA, EDUARDO 1988 *The Great Temple of the Aztecs: Treasures of Tenochtitlan.* Thames and Hudson, New York.

NICHOLSON, H. B., WITH ELOISE QUIÑONES KEBER 1983 *Art of Aztec Mexico: Treasures of Tenochtitlan.* National Gallery of Art, Washington, D.C.

PASZTORY, ESTHER 1983 *Aztec Art.* Harry N. Abrams, Inc., New York.

TOWNSEND, RICHARD F. 1979 State and Cosmos in the Art of Tenochtitlan. *Studies in Pre-Columbian Art and Archaeology* No. 20. Dumbarton Oaks, Washington, D.C.

CHAPTER 9: THE FALL OF THE EMPIRE

Hernán Cortés and Bernal Díaz del Castillo give us the Spanish version of the Conquest. For the native version, see Sahagún's book 12, which has also been issued as a separate publication by Arthur Anderson and Charles Dibble, and see Miguel León-Portilla's *The Broken Spears,* which combines Sahagún's account with several others.

ANDERSON, ARTHUR J.O. AND CHARLES E. DIBBLE 1978 *The War of Conquest: How It Was Waged Here in Mexico.* University of Utah Press, Salt Lake City.

LEÓN-PORTILLA, MIGUEL 1962 *The Broken Spears: The Aztec Account of the Conquest of Mexico.* Beacon Press, Boston.

INDEX

PICTURE CREDITS

AUTHOR'S ACKNOWLEDGMENTS

One thing my study of Aztec history and Aztec painted manuscripts has taught me is that all peoples have different stories about the past. In Aztec times, there was not just one canonical history that the elders told, and recorded pictorially, about their origins and rise to greatness. Instead, there were many stories, each with its variations and embellishments, that corroborated, disagreed with, and complemented each other. The stories reflected different times, interests, and purposes.

When my friend and colleague, Jerry Sabloff, asked me to write a book on the Aztecs, I thought about all the other books that have been written on the Aztecs and the different perspectives they offer. Many are superb and insightful accounts of the Aztec empire and people, which continue to be important in shaping our view of Aztec culture. As excellent as these books are, however, none puts the focus where I would put it, and none tells the Aztec story the way I would. I thank Jerry for encouraging me to tell my own story of the Aztecs.

This is a story that emphasizes the patterns of thought behind Aztec ways and that tries to make sense of the Aztecs in their own terms. More distinctively, it draws deeply from the words of the Aztecs and Spaniards who in the 16th century wrote about the Mexican past. As much as possible, I have quoted directly from the original authors, so that the reader hears the ancient Aztec voices and the words of the chroniclers, even though they arrive filtered by translation and time.

This book treats those aspects of Aztec culture that I felt an educated layperson or nonspecialist should know and would find most interesting. I wrote the book for my father, Russell Hill, and three sisters—Natalie Zung, Cathy May, and Patricia

Banks, all of whom have a somewhat distant interest in Aztec Mexico. The question that arose at the beginning and throughout my writing was: What would my sister Cathy want to know about the Aztecs?

Thanks are due to many people. First, I and all other Aztec specialists owe an immense debt of gratitude to Arthur Anderson and Charles Dibble, who for nearly 30 years labored to translate Bernardino de Sahagún's *Florentine Codex* from Nahuatl into English. They have made Sahagún an even clearer window onto the Aztec world. Miguel León-Portilla, Doris Heyden, and the late Fernando Horcasitas are three other fine editors who have given us the chroniclers' words in translation. During this project, a number of colleagues came to my aid with advice and information; for this, I am grateful to Patricia Anawalt, Frances Berdan, Susan Evans, Mary Hodge, Cecelia Klein, and Dana Leibsohn. Other colleagues and many institutions generously provided or helped with photographs; thank you Emily Umberger, Ross Parmenter, and Carol Callaway. And John Verano knows how much I value his gently barbed critiques of my phrasings.

At St. Remy Press, I am grateful to Carolyn Jackson's fine editorial and production team, especially Alfred LeMaitre, Philippe Arnoldi, Chris Jackson, and Jennifer Meltzer. I thank Dumbarton Oaks, in the person of its director, Angeliki Laiou, for research leave in 1993-94 that allowed me to concentrate on this book in the summer of 1993.

Elizabeth H. Boone
Washington, D.C.